only spring

on mourning the
death of my son

GORDON LIVINGSTON, M.D.

foreword by Mark Helprin

HarperSanFrancisco
A Division of HarperCollins*Publishers*

Permissions begin on p. 232 and constitute a continuation of the copyright page.

Frontispiece photograph by Andrew Livingston.

FIRST EDITION

Book design by Claudia Smelser

Livingston, Gordon.
    Only spring : on mourning the death of my son/
    Gordon Livingston.—1st ed.
    p.   cm.
    ISBN 0–06–251060–6 (cloth alk. paper)
    ISBN 0–06–251061–4 (pbk. alk. paper)
    1. Livingston, Lucas Scott, 1985–1992. 2. Acute myelocytic
    leukemia in children—Patients—Family relationships.
    3. Livingston, Gordon. 4. Bereavement—Case studies.
    5. Children—Death—Psychological aspects—Case studies.
    6. Fathers—Diaries. I. Title.
RJ416.A25L56   1995
362. 1'989299419—dc20
[B]   94–31538
                                        CIP

95 96 97 98 99 ❖ RRD(H) 10 9 8 7 6 5 4 3 2 1
This edition is printed on acid-free paper that meets the American National Standards Institute Z39.48 Standard.

For Clare and Emily,
whose love and courage
shone always upon Lucas
and now light a path for me.

contents

in memorium

Yet, oh stricken soul, remember, oh remember,
How of human days he lived the better part.
April came to him and never chill December
Breathed its killing chills upon his head or heart.

Doomed to know not winter, only spring,
A being trod the flowery April for a while,
Took his fill of music, joy of thought and seeing,
Came and stayed and went, nor ever ceased to smile.

Came and stayed and went, and now, when all is finished,
You alone have crossed the melancholy stream.
Yours the pangs, but his, oh his, the undiminished
Undecaying gladness, undeparted dream.

All that life contains of torture, toil and treason,
Shame, dishonor, death, to him were but a name.
Here, a boy, he dwelt through all the singing seasons
And ere the day of sorrow, departed as he came.

Robert Louis Stevenson

lucas

Nothing is as inappropriate as the death of a child, nothing makes the universe seem quite so bitter and senseless, nothing so shakes the throne of God. For the child who is taken has not had a life of disappointment that death will clear. He has not had time to reflect upon the inadequacies of natural and social systems savage and unkind enough to require the death of children. He has not been trained in theology or in physics or in ten-thousand-year myths, and although he may believe in the afterworld as no adult might dare, child-like acceptance of things barely grasped, the sweetest faith and the most fragile, is likely to get him no further upon the test than children's plastic tools are likely to shape a house when applied to the real hardness and weight of wood.

He has not had lessons in courage, building it over years and decades as he learns to risk, to lose, to come back, and to win. He has not seen and understood things that are almost indistinguishable from miracles, things suggesting that the world is not merely mechanical, that we do not understand the simplest and most important questions, and that, therefore, we cannot rule out the hints of transcendence that flow to us in the greatest volume at the peak of our powers and in the strength of our youth, or, if we latch on to the practice of it, even as we age.

He has not had, for example, the chance to divine in the music of Mozart what Mozart apprehended of a finer world of obvious and absolute perfection. In not having had the opportunity to study beauty and its relations, he has not been shown that perfection is possible, that a point of aim exists, that something there is of promise and order.

He has not learned either to endure pain or to understand that all pain comes to an end. He has not had his fill of life. He cannot say, "I have done right, and my task is complete." He still fears the darkness, and monsters, and ghosts. He has no one to carry forward for him in this world, and no one to care for him in the next, for in leaving his father and mother behind he cannot enjoy even the illusion that they will be waiting to take him in their arms, much less the chance that it will be so.

The "inappropriateness," in which the sense of the universe is undone, is unbearable. And yet it and other terrors must be borne often enough. This is the story of Gordon Livingston and his son Lucas—the father a man of unusual courage, intellect, and honesty, and the son an innocent child barely out of infancy, with the face and demeanor of an angel. And when the other angel came, it chose to wrestle not with the fit, old soldier, who could draw upon his memories, resurrecting the old patterns of tenacity and defiance to give death a run for its money until almost the very end, but with the boy, who did not even know the terms of the game.

The cruelties of the world are often associated with sin, but this cruelty was visited solely by nature, which, by nature, is itself without sin. What kind of God would allow the world He created to act so coldly upon the most innocent and vulnerable, especially when the father was standing by, having lived a full life, ready to die for his son a thousand times?

The answer is a God who, in ravishing you, eviscerates your faith and trust in him while at the same time leaving you with nothing but the hope that He exists and will in another world extend to you the missing pieces in His puzzle of mercy.

If God is continually testing us, then I imagine that one of His tests is to take our measure by making us choose between defense of our children and acceptance of His rule. I imagine further that the story of Abraham and Isaac was a bit of disinformation, artfully placed to cull unctuous sycophants from the legions of good souls. For, as far as I can see (and I admit that it might not be very far), the game is not worth the candle if God actually expects us to acquiesce in the sacrifice of His own angels. I expect that He does not. The answer was clear to Gordon Livingston: he would not. He would, if necessary, war against God to save his son.

I would do the same. Probably you would do the same. How could God not favor such a decision, given all that He has shown us of what is precious, right, and good? How could He not?

And yet, though Lucas passed all the tests of innocence, and all those around him passed the tests of devotion and courage, he was taken nonetheless, and he died when he was six years old.

Drawn into the maelstrom of his sickness, dying, and death, the father recorded what passed by him, producing in the chapters that chronicle these events the most moving document I have ever read, not least because his reflections, like an intricate and monumental prayer, were part of the impossible struggle to save his son, and, afterward, to guide him in the blind world into which he was drawn, to cut a path for him by penetrating the mysteries, rather than by merely preceding him, the privilege accorded to most fathers.

Whether Lucas rose into a world of light or was taken with a roar into waves of speeding darkness as if into the deep ocean, he went alone. The way I see it, he is either clasped tightly to the breast of God, or there is no God. One way or another, he has given his father, and in some respects all of us, a great gift. He has made death a prospect of fulfillment, an excitement, for what greater need is there but to find the lost child, or at least to chance that one may find him? If you were on a ship battered by immense waves (and, believe me, you are) that swept your child from your arms would you not (given that you had no others for whom to remain) throw yourself into the deep, hoping for the chance that in the vast black ocean you might grab onto him? Comforted just to know that you would suffer the same fate?

And if you had to remain, to protect others, would you not dream all your life of the day when, your responsibilities over, you would finally get to the sea?

That Lucas Livingston has given to those who love him the gift that death is now an opportunity to make things whole, to fulfill the most sacred duty, to chance an even greater reward than that of eternal life, to find the lost child, is why, in my estimation, he is a saint. I use that word in the Jewish sense, meaning someone who enjoys neither title nor privilege nor even earthly recognition but is, rather, someone who is—who must be—beloved of God.

At the end of his narrative everything but one thing is stripped from Gordon Livingston—indeed, everything but one thing is stripped from the reader of the story—everything but one thing remains inviolable and, apparently, invincible. And that is love. For in the end this is the story of a parent's love for a child, a father's love for his son, and no greater story has ever been told. Perhaps if we are left with nothing more than this, it will have been enough, but is it not intriguing that the story may yet continue? For it may. And if it does, then Lucas Livingston will, somehow, someday, take his father's hand.

Mark Helprin
August 1994

acknowledgments

Some of those to whom I owe special thanks are mentioned in the pages to come; many are not. These omissions are inevitable in the record of one person's thoughts and feelings at a time of great distress and limited vision. I am sorry for any such oversights, which do not reflect the gratitude I feel to all who have given so much to me and my family.

Among those who were instrumental in bringing this journal to publication are David Talbot and Gary Kamiya of the *San Francisco Examiner,* who were the first to believe that Lucas's story might mean something to others. I am indebted also to my agent, Gareth Esersky, and to my editors, Caroline Pincus and Luann Rouff, who, with exceptional kindness, led me through the process of assembling these words into a book.

Apart from the many family members and friends who have supported and continue to support us, there are a multitude of people we do not know whose prayers, condolences, and caring have meant more than I can say.

Finally, a special thankfulness extends to our friend Janet Klarsfeld, who died one week before this writing while awaiting her own bone marrow transplant and whose generous wish it was that contributions in her memory be directed to Lucas's memorial fund.

C. S. Lewis said, "We read to know that we are not alone." So also do we write.

Gordon Livingston
Columbia, Maryland
October 1994

introduction

The life of every man is a diary in which
he means to write one story, and writes
another; and his humblest hour is when he
compares the volume it is with what he
vowed to make it.

J. M. Barrie

This is the story of the life and death of my son.

Lucas, at six, was my youngest child but not the
first to die. With the bitter irony that fate sometimes
reserves for those who dare count themselves happy,
his older brother, Andrew, took his own life at age
twenty-two, just eight months before Lucas was diagnosed with leukemia.

When he died from complications of his treatment,
Lucas took with him the last vestiges of my youth but
left behind the memory of the purest love, given and
received, that I have ever known. Though much of this
story reads like a nightmare, it has become to me a
sort of healing dream that carries within it meanings I
never thought to see.

During his brief time upon this earth, Lucas brought us happiness beyond all calculation. When he was seized by leukemia, I was already keeping a journal in which I continued to write as we struggled to save him. He underwent six hospitalizations for chemotherapy and, finally, a bone marrow transplant with me as the donor. During that time, Lucas taught us about the power of the human spirit and what it means to be a family. It is this special and permanent gift that I have tried to capture in the pages that follow.

The death of a child is a violation of the natural order of life. Nothing in our experience prepares us as parents for such a catastrophe. When the death results from a prolonged illness, we are left with the excruciating memories of alternating periods of hope and despair, culminating in the horror created by the sights and sounds of modern technological medicine: the incessant hissing of a respirator, the alarming beeps of monitors and intravenous pumps, and the green lines on a cathode-ray tube that rivet our attention until the end, when they finally signal us that the struggle is over.

One in twenty thousand. The numbers still haunt me. This is the approximate incidence of childhood leukemia in the general population. Such minuscule odds force one to confront the questions of all who suffer an improbable disaster: "Why me? Why my child?" The answer, of course, heartless in its simplicity, is "Why not?" Implied in these questions is our struggle to understand the terrible things that happen to us. Through some combination of acceptance and denial, we learn to live with the knowledge of our own mortality. A child's death, however, out of sequence and without discernible meaning, touches our deepest fears about the randomness of the universe and tests whatever beliefs we may harbor about the guiding hand of a just God.

The loss of my son has illuminated for me the true definition of love: the giving of oneself, body and spirit, to another. His death, like that of any child, is a story of withered hopes and unfulfilled dreams. In this book I have tried to capture a few remembered strains of the brief, glad music of his life. These are all I have of him now, and they comfort me even as they break my heart.

The story, then, has two parts. One concerns the physical and psychological struggle of a family with a child caught suddenly in the grip of an awful disease and the requirement to submit to the painful, and ultimately futile, attempts to save him. The second part, ever incomplete, chronicles the attempt to grieve, to find meaning in our loss, to distill hope from anguish, and to validate the lesson of Lucas's life and death: that it is our ability to love, still and again, that is the ultimate act of faith.

diagnosis

In moments when I try to recall what my
life was like when last I was happy, I think
of the Paratrooper ride on the boardwalk
at Rehoboth, Delaware. Lucas sat on the
inside so that the whirling force pressed
him against me. As we spun around and
around, we were thrown into the sky for a
brief glimpse of the beach and the dark sea
beyond. In the next instant we plunged
earthward, toward Clare and Emily, who
smiled and waved as we rushed past to
start again our climb to the heavens. Lucas
laughed in delight, holding on to me, excited and safe. When we finally stopped,
he rested in my arms a moment before
looking up to ask, "Please, Dad, can we do
it again?" And so we would. I remember
wishing, even as I knew it could not be,
that the ride would go on forever.

On Tuesday Clare took Lucas to our pediatrician for a persistent runny nose. Scott Strahlman thought he had sinusitis and started him on an antibiotic. Because he looked pale, Scott ordered a blood count and called me an hour later to suggest we take him to the Hematology Clinic at Johns Hopkins for "further evaluation."

"Scott," I asked, "what's wrong?"

"His white count is high and he's anemic. I'd like them to have a look at his blood smear. No reason to panic."

But I knew there was. On the drive to Baltimore, Clare said, "I'm scared."

"Me too" was the best I could manage. We could not bring ourselves to say the word that so terrified us.

After microscopic examination of his blood smear, a young physician called me into an exam room and announced simply, "Lucas has leukemia." Even though I thought I had prepared myself, I was devastated. I began to perspire, became nauseated, and thought I might faint. It felt like a death sentence. The doctor then continued in a businesslike way to talk about arrangements for immediate hospitalization. With my seemingly healthy son playing with his mother in the next room, I naively asked, "Why does he need to be in the hospital?" A look of surprise crossed the doctor's face and his thought was transparent: How could a physician ask such an incredibly dumb question? He patiently explained the need for a bone marrow examination, a lumbar puncture to look at Lucas's spinal fluid, and further testing to determine the cell type—

which would dictate the chemotherapy protocol. It was too soon to say anything about treatment or prognosis. They would know more in a few days. What I remember thinking is that this man was in a specialty in which the delivering of bad news was routine. He was doing his job in a straightforward way, conveying neither optimism nor pessimism since he had no grounds for either. What did I expect from him? Not false hope, certainly. Not reassurance or predictions. I realized that what I wanted was some understanding of what it was like for a father to face the news that his vibrantly healthy son, who a few hours ago seemed to have an inconsequential cold, carried within him a malignant disease that might kill him—and that it was now my job to convey that verdict to his mother and eleven-year-old sister. Our lives were being turned upside down. Whatever happened, we would never be the same. What could this doctor have done? He was a stranger, sympathetic I guessed, though his face revealed little. Could he have touched my shoulder, said that he understood my shock and disorientation? Or did he feel what I thought I would have felt in his place: "Thank God this is happening to him and not me."

I told Clare the diagnosis and we controlled our emotions enough to explain to Lucas the need for the hospital and the tests. He was unafraid and only needed reassurance that we would stay with him. We went to the eighth floor, the Pediatric Oncology ward. He tolerated bravely the IV, the spinal tap, and the bone marrow aspiration from his hip, which, of course, in accordance with Murphy's Law, required several attempts and the efforts of two different doctors before enough marrow was obtained. As I sat beside him through this, holding his hand, resting my head against his, he looked at me and, sensing my own ordeal, said, "I love you, Dad."

The evening of the day of diagnosis, I went to pick up Emily, who had come home from school with a friend. When I told her of the leukemia she began to cry. Though I was having trouble maintaining my own equilibrium, I said we were confident that the treatment would work and that, in spite of our fears, we all had to convey to Lucas an optimistic attitude. She asked that we stop at a drugstore on the way to the hospital to buy him a stuffed animal.

After an endless day of waiting, we were told that testing of the bone marrow showed that he had acute lymphocytic leukemia, T-cell type, which carries an intermediate risk in terms of "cure" percentages, somewhere around 50 percent—neither the best nor the worst. We signed permission for chemotherapy with multiple drugs that were to be started that night. Meanwhile, he was going to need an "infusaport" surgically implanted in his chest to avoid the necessity of repeated needle punctures to draw blood and inject the chemotherapeutic agents. I stayed with him in the operating room until he was asleep. When I left him there, so vulnerable and facing this terrible cancer, I felt something close to panic. Before joining Clare in the family waiting room, and not yet willing to burden her with my fears, I went into a stairwell and wept. I couldn't bear the thought of losing him; even the procedures we had put him through in the last twenty-four hours were hardly bearable for us as adults who understood why they were necessary. What must they be like for him, uncomprehending but trusting his mom and dad to take care of him? So begins my free fall into helplessness. Where will it end?

He came through the surgery well but vomited until there was nothing left, then retched with the dry heaves. The anti-nausea drugs they tried didn't control it.

DECEMBER 21, 1991

This evening, Dr. Friedman, the attending oncologist, came in to tell us that further tests on Lucas's blood had yielded markers more suggestive of acute myelocytic leukemia, the type with the lowest cure rate and the one that may require a bone marrow transplant. He, of course, was apologetic and embarrassed by the initial mistake in diagnosis and explained the circumstances in excruciating and complex detail. Once more we have to absorb worse news on top of bad and try to muster our dwindling reserves of optimism because our attitudes seem so crucial to sustain a healing presence and maintain both Lucas's and Emily's morale. Thanks to Clare's strength, we have been able to interpret all this awful information in the best possible light. Her reaction was, "So they say he has a 40 percent chance of survival. When hasn't Lucas been in the upper 40 percent of anything?" We believe that Lucas will survive, whatever the odds, and that this terrible episode will draw all of us together in a way that will strengthen and dignify our lives. We can be discouraged and frightened, but we will not be defeated by this disease.

Today we brought him home from the hospital. His white count is down as expected from the chemo, but he has no fever and is playing with his five-year-old cousin, Clare, and the many gifts he has received. His hospital room overflowed and it took six adults to carry them all to the car. Clare's sisters, Ann and Julie, have come from Atlanta and my daughter, Nina, a medical student at Harvard, is here from Boston. This is the longest night of the year; a full moon shines in my window as I write this; and soon Lucas, Clare, and I will again sleep together in the family bed.

Nina brought me a quote from Henry James:

> We work in the dark—we do what we can—we give what we have. Our doubt is our passion and our passion is our task. The rest is the madness of art.

DECEMBER 24, 1991

Christmas Eve. One week since diagnosis and I seem to be caught in a sort of determined denial as I think of Lucas's illness. I find it hard to get myself to read the material on leukemia that they gave us at the hospital. Nina has some hematology texts that I also have no desire to read. I think I am just choosing to believe that the discouraging statistics don't apply to him; he's going to make it and that's that. Clare and I have already planned to organize the next couple of years around his treatment in all its complexity. We cannot, will not, accept the thought of anything but a good outcome.

Lucas runs about the house now, putting out milk and cookies for Santa and leaving him a laboriously written thank-you letter. We've gone overboard, if such a thing is possible, on the presents and I can't wait for tomorrow morning. Seeing him looking so happy and excited is a gift beyond measure. That initial five days in the hospital renders all other time intensely pleasurable. The bandage where his infusaport is implanted is a reminder of reality, but the absence of fever and only a few episodes of nausea bode well. Surely his specialness extends to his response to treatment.

Lots of people came by today to drop off presents and visit. In contrast to our largely lonely grief over Andrew's death, this threat to Lucas has mobilized all kinds of support. These include offers from my colleagues to donate vacation time to me, welcome gifts in view of the many trips to the hospital that 1992 doubtless holds in store.

I feel unexpectedly peaceful, probably because we're at home. I just hope the energy- and morale-sapping effects of the treatment will not wear us down. I know this experience will change all our lives. Maybe I'll even come out of it believing in God.

DECEMBER 28, 1991

It feels like the first onslaught of the hurricane has passed over us and we rest for a moment in the eye of the storm. Lucas has largely recovered from the side effects of the initial chemotherapy. His white count should be about at the nadir, which makes him very vulnerable to infection, but still he has no fever. Most of the day he's in good spirits, laughing and playing with his Christmas toys, including his favorite, a working old-fashioned telephone.

Knowing what lies ahead, the repeated chemo treatments and hospitalizations, I feel oddly unafraid. Denial it may be, but I simply can't conceive of this whole ordeal as anything other than a test of faith and fortitude that we all must pass. I do have an impulse to bargain with whatever God there may be to let this child live and grow. It is at once the most selfish and selfless of prayers, even if I am uncertain where to direct it. It comforts me to know of the firmly religious people we have heard from who are asking God's help in ways in which they truly believe. I hope that their certain faith redeems my poor agnosticism when the Almighty weighs the fate of my son.

I am left with only my love for him and every father's hope for his child's full and happy life. I hate the thought of putting him through the pain and sickness that offer his only chance, but, as I never really could with Andrew's illness, I find myself able to experience this ordeal with Lucas. I fear most a time when that awful free fall of helplessness returns. For the moment, while I can hold him, trusting and painless, in my arms, I am happy.

DECEMBER 30, 1991

Lucas became lethargic yesterday, spiked a fever last night, and had to be taken back to the hospital. He received transfusions and today was more alert. His infusaport is not usable yet, but he was very brave about the needle sticks for blood cultures. It surprises us that he can tolerate this pain, given the way we have always indulged him. He has a certain inner toughness that contrasts to his gentle, loving demeanor.

I lay in the hospital bed with him awhile this evening and we both fell asleep. When I touch him I imagine my strength flowing into him—perhaps the best transfusion of all. I know that Clare and Emily have the same feeling, and I can't believe that this won't result in an accelerated destruction of the malignancy. We also need to teach Lucas to visualize the "good cells attacking the bad cells" so that, with the help of the chemotherapy, he can heal himself. My awful initial fear of the disease has disappeared and has been replaced by anger and determination. Clare's quiet confidence sustains us all.

JANUARY 4, 1992

We welcomed in the new year by crowding at midnight into a small storage room at the end of the Oncology ward to watch the fireworks over the Inner Harbor in Baltimore. Another family with a four-year-old boy came in and we jockeyed the IV poles around so all could see.

The hospitalization turned into six days because Lucas kept running fevers. Since all cultures were negative, he probably had some type of virus, but they gave him a variety of antibiotics anyway. We finally got him out, though he has to go back for more chemotherapy in three days. Then everyone in the family gets blood drawn to see if any of us is a suitable donor for a bone marrow transplant. Emily has a one in four chance of qualifying, the rest of us much less; she is so hoping that she will be a match.

When the chemotherapy started I had this conversation with Lucas:

"Luke, you know one of the things that will happen here is that the medicine will probably make your hair fall out. It'll just be for a little while, though, then it will grow back."

Lucas said, "I don't want to be bald." Then he cried and I held him.

Today his hair started coming out. The part that went first was the back where his head rubs against the pillow. He can't see this bald spot, but when he went to the bathroom he backed against the door and felt the skin on his head touch the cold surface. He immediately asked for a hand mirror so he could see and now accepts that it really is going to happen. He worries what the kids in his kindergarten class will think and watches the Charlie Brown videotape about leukemia again, especially the part where the little girl is teased by one of the other children for being bald. We talk about hats he can wear and tell him his teacher has prepared all the kids so they won't be surprised or make fun of him.

Emily and I had a talk tonight about the meaning of all this:

EMILY: It's not fair.
ME: That's right, babe, it's not.
EMILY: Why Lucas?
ME: I don't know. I ask myself that all the time.

JANUARY 9, 1992

We all had our blood drawn to determine if any of us could serve as a transplant donor. When Clare's turn came, the venipuncture technician had difficulty finding a vein and stuck her repeatedly. Lucas, who has endured many needle sticks uncomplainingly, cupped Clare's face in his hands and said, "Mom, I'm sorry they had to stick you so much. I'm sorry they hurt you."

JANUARY 11, 1992

No match. The good news is that Lucas's latest bone marrow aspiration showed less than 1 percent malignant cells, so he's in remission. Now he will be assaulted with a week's worth of chemotherapy. It's hard not to be disappointed that a transplant from one of us won't be possible, but seeing him feeling well, watching tapes, playing games, going to the playroom, and even eating pizza is wonderfully uplifting to our spirits. I cannot believe that any force in the universe would put me here to watch my little boy die—an irrational belief, to be sure, since it happens all the time. Yet I am sustained by a residual faith in fairness that I refuse to relinquish. I feel also the need, as do we all, to communicate confidence to Lucas in every possible way to help him heal. He's now learned to swallow pills and take eyedrops three times a day. His infusaport spares him the pain of the needle sticks. Even with his hair covering his pillow, he retains his sweet smile and mischievous sense of humor. I think we will look back on this greatest crisis of our lives with pride and renewed faith in the power of love.

JANUARY 12, 1992

I remembered today reading the accident report from a couple of years ago about the DC-10 that lost all hydraulic power over Iowa when a fan blade fractured on the rear engine. This left the crew with frozen controls and no way to steer the airplane except by differential power on the remaining two engines underneath the wings. This is a little like steering a sailboat without the rudder. Though the situation seemed hopeless, the crew kept their heads and gingerly and erratically, going in circle after circle, got the plane down at the Sioux City airport. They caught a wingtip on landing and crashed, but two-thirds of the passengers survived. I'm feeling like a member of that crew these days, my life suddenly thrown out of control, trying to salvage the situation with what's left—faith, optimism, and chemotherapy. Clare seems to me more like the pilot, asking the good questions and spending the nights in the hospital with Lucas. His attitude is playful, energetic. His beautiful blond hair is mostly gone. Still he soldiers on, too brave and good to die. There's an old saying in aviation that "any landing you can walk away from is a good landing." I believe that somehow we'll all walk away from this one.

JANUARY 15, 1992

The questions from Lucas are starting: "What can you see when you're dead?" To Emily's reply that you go to heaven he asked, "Would Andrew be there?" I felt the ground crumbling beneath my feet. Maybe that was the point of Andrew's death—so that Lucas won't have to be alone. *Oh God, no.*

JANUARY 18, 1992

After four days out of the hospital, Lucas developed a fever to 102.6 and was readmitted this morning. He asked Clare yesterday if people die of leukemia. We've decided to respond as if there were no possibility of his not surviving this illness. Everything we say or do with him, and each other, assumes that he will recover. Somewhere in the back of my mind, of course, lurks the fear beyond all fears, but I want our communication to him to reflect unambivalent optimism—not far from our true attitude at that. He must believe wholly in recovery if he is to have the maximum chance. If we are wrong, we will face the unimaginable task of helping him die when we have to, not before.

Dr. Bob Norton, the attending oncologist and bone marrow transplant expert, said out of the blue today that I have enough matching surface markers on my white cells to justify further testing as a possible donor. The odds are against my being suitable, but even the chance is exciting. One of the things they do is mix my lymphocytes with his to find out if they can get along. Oh, what a gift that would be! The alternative is continued chemotherapy.

Lucas's spirits are good. I go home each night with Emily and take her to school; Clare remains at the hospital. I think this is called coping: believing in Lucas, ourselves, and a merciful God—with whom I expect to become better acquainted in the coming months.

JANUARY 21, 1992

After spending twenty-one of the last thirty-four days in the hospital, Lucas is home. The remnants of his hair are blonder than ever and he is energetic, though he has lost weight and is frail-looking compared with his former robust self. He reminds me now more of Andrew when he was Lucas's age.

It now looks like the oncologists are leaning toward several rounds of chemotherapy in preference to an "autologous" transplant, that is, a reinfusion of his own treated marrow. I can't decide how I feel about that, but find it hard to imagine not accepting their recommendation. Perhaps it's prideful to believe that he'll do well, whatever the treatment, but his good response so far encourages this attitude.

I remain immersed in what I've come to think of as "the literature of hope"—Bernie Siegel, Norman Cousins, the Simontons, et al. Right now I'm reading Erma Bombeck's book on kids with cancer. We need more than ever to retain our senses of humor.

We think all the time about what more we can do to support his spirit and perhaps thereby increase the probability of healing. We're hoping to do so by creating an environment so filled with determination that he inhales it with the air he breathes. Clare has a plenitude of this strength in her gentle way and will probably be the main instrument of its transmission to him.

JANUARY 22, 1992

I have always thought of my life as an amazing and ultimately joyful journey. Now in the space of a few months I have had to face the death of my oldest son and leukemia in my youngest. I find myself trying to understand these events. Have I been indulged for so long only to be ruined now? Is this a test? If so, what must I do to pass? Is it absurd to imagine a purpose behind all this?

Lucas has been home for a week. His blood counts have bottomed out for four days and don't seem to be recovering. Is this just the expected suppression from the chemo or could he have relapsed? We find out the day after tomorrow when the next bone marrow aspiration is done—and when my blood is drawn to see if there is any chance for a match close enough to justify a transplant. He seems pale but in good spirits, playing a lot of Nintendo and watching the Charles Schulz videotape about leukemia. I simply cannot conceive of life without him, even as the possibility terrifies me. I hold him close, he sleeps between us, and time is marked by the daily lab numbers on which hang all our fates. I think I'm developing something akin to religious faith, some basic belief that we are put here for a reason other than to grieve one loss after another.

Last night the snow fell, and early this morning I plowed our church parking lot. *I will strike any bargain, God, if you will spare my son.*

Lucas has had ten wonderful days without fever and out of the hospital. His counts bottomed out and bounced back, and tomorrow we take him in for an admission for more chemotherapy. His marrow was still in remission two days ago. He's had a couple of days in school and even had a friend come home with him this afternoon. We were naturally concerned about how the other kids would react to his baldness. He wore a hat to school but soon took it off and got only a few curious stares from his well-briefed class-mates. I asked his teacher, Michelle Kupiec, how things were going. She said, "While he was in the hospital the children were very worried. I overheard conversations among them. They said, 'I hope he comes back soon' and 'Will he remember us?' On the day he returned I was nervous, wanting everything to go well. He arrived wearing a bright red baseball cap with his name written on it in blue lettering. He was so brave, so beautiful, so innocent! He told us that he had a magic button inside of him and lifted up his shirt so the kids could look at his infusaport."

Barbara Siddle Bolin, a psychologist and friend, has started to teach Lucas visualization techniques, and he has adopted the "Pac-Man" image of the good cells devouring the bad ones.

JANUARY 31, 1992

Lucas went back into the hospital today for what we hope will be a reasonably easy course of chemo. The observation in some of the cancer literature about this disease occurring in people within a year after a serious loss inevitably brings Andrew's death to mind. Is Lucas's illness somehow an expression of his grieving? I find myself angry at the possibility that Andrew's killing himself played a role in this. Clare responds that this is a time for forgiveness. *So, it's okay, Andrew. I know you meant no one else harm, least of all your little brother. How I wish you were here, though, to help us all through this.*

FEBRUARY 5, 1992

It is a strange thing, this fear that hangs over us like a sword of Damocles. I go about my life in good spirits, but lurking in the back of my consciousness is the awful "40 percent"—the quoted cure rate for this type of leukemia. He is doing so well, completed his recent chemotherapy course without the expected fever, and has been going to school for the last two days. He *must,* with his cheery, energetic outlook, be in a different statistical category. If there is anything at all to the "attitudinal healing" movement, then his recovery seems assured. Barbara is still working with him on visualization, and his response to chemo, both in terms of remission and side effects, has been wonderful. From all of this we draw the hope that seems so necessary to get him well. And yet I can't help but wonder if we are being fools in the face of onrushing catastrophe. I rebuke myself for what seems like a lack of faith but find it hard to relinquish my habitual skepticism. I'm so afraid that I am weakened in my efforts to help him. My prayers, such as they are, reek with the fraudulence of a battlefield conversion. Yet I would do anything, promise anything, sell my soul to either God or the devil to purchase my son's life. If this is hypocrisy, then so be it.

FEBRUARY 11, 1992

Today Clare and I met with the oncologists and they recommended that Lucas get a bone marrow transplant with me as the donor. I'm "one-antigen incompatible"—my lymphocytes match his except for one surface antigen. Amid the myriad of numbers, the one that sticks is that he has about a 66 percent chance of cure if the marrow takes and the complications, especially "graft versus host disease" (probability greater than 80 percent), are manageable. Bob Norton, the transplant specialist, was confident, and all seemed to agree that this is Lucas's best hope. If I could be the instrument of his recovery, I would ask nothing more of my life. The transplant feels like the right thing to do in a way that the reliance on chemotherapy alone didn't. We have such confidence in his and our ability to overcome this cancer that the most aggressive (and shortest) course is appealing. In six months we may be able to breathe freely again; in two years with no relapse they consider him cured. We're waiting now for his blood counts from the last chemo treatments to rebound; then it's into the hospital for the transplant—probably early March.

FEBRUARY 12, 1992

The more time I have to consider the implications of this turn of events, the more they become both frightening and exciting. Lucas seems so fragile without his hair, so pale because of the anemia. Through it all he is trusting, although he has his own doubts and fears ("Can the bad cells kill you?"). It seems like the transplant, while potentially curative, is also forcing the issue sooner than relying on the chemotherapy would. We know he can tolerate the drugs and maybe they alone can cure him. By plunging into the transplant, trying to "cross the immune barrier" as Bob Norton puts it, we seem to be challenging one of life's elemental proscriptions. We are asking his body to accept my marrow and vice versa, hoping that my transplanted immune cells will not irretrievably damage his vital organs. There is something spiritually appealing about putting this part of me into him—if it works.

Just because I feel so close to him in every way does not mean that he can live with my lymphocytes. If he does not, can I ever forgive myself the time I might have had with him on the chemo regimen, whatever its eventual outcome? It is probably just as well for our sanity that we cannot foretell the future. Or what would pass for courage? I pray a lot these days, groping for both the words and some vision of whom or what I am addressing.

Lucas speaks to me now of life and death. "Why does God make you grow slowly?" he asks, and I wonder if the word "old" has been omitted. He looks at the backyard covered with snow and asks if the trees are lonely and cold without their leaves. He lost a tooth last night and is happy at this milestone. But I think he feels the shadow of his mortality when he looks in the mirror and sees the white-blond remnants of his beautiful hair. *Let my bone marrow be worthy of his spirit.* It is Valentine's Day and I love him so. The unknown future rolls toward us and I am ready—but afraid.

We received word today that the bone marrow transplant will take place on March nineteenth—our wedding anniversary. This date seems a good omen. Bob Norton says he prefers to "harvest" my marrow under epidural block, the same anesthesia Clare had in delivering both Emily and Lucas. In a way I suppose that this is as close as I'll get to the childbirth experience. Waiting for it to happen I feel uniquely valuable, with a greater sense of purpose than I could have imagined at this stage of my life. The fact that the gift I am to give is not really of my making seems fitting. The best things in life, I am convinced, happen with a naturalness that approaches inevitability. I hope a miracle is in the offing and I am its unworthy but indispensable instrument. If this is the hand of God directing our fates, then I must believe in His power—and mercy.

FEBRUARY 23, 1992

We now have the schedule: outpatient workup for Lucas and me from March 3 to March 6; placement of the Hickman catheter, a central venous line, on March 6; admission for the chemotherapy to kill his bone marrow on March 9; transplant on March 19. Not only is that date our anniversary, it is also the Catholic feast day of St. Joseph, Jesus' father. These coincidences augur well in our minds. We are writing all who have expressed concern about Lucas, asking that they send photos of themselves to place on the wall of his hospital room.

Emily, Lucas, and I went for a long bike ride today. The temperature was near seventy degrees, and it was so wonderful to have him sitting in the seat behind me, chatting, pointing out the ducks, and begging to race Emily, which we finally did in a rush down the hill near home. He is completely unself-conscious about his straggly hair. His energy and morale are up and so are mine.

Lucas asks me, "Does God hold all the planets and stars together?" "Yes," I say. "When you're dead, do you get to see him do this?" he wonders. "Yes," I answer. "He must be really big!" says Lucas. The subject of death is on his mind as we await the transplant. When I think of the things that have frightened me in this life, they seem as nothing compared to the fear I feel now.

I carry a nearly palpable dread inside me and know that Clare does also. It invades my dreams and several times I have awakened short of breath. Our decision to answer Lucas's questions honestly, but convey un-equivocal optimism, still seems to me the only way to see him (and ourselves) through this ordeal.

FEBRUARY 25, 1992

At a meeting I attended recently, someone said that "forgiveness is one of those things you can't imagine doing until the moment you do it." It was also the theme of last week's sermon at church. We find our-selves trying to tie up loose ends, practical and emo-tional, as we approach March 19.

He will be in the hospital at least six weeks and Clare will be with him while I take Emily back and forth to school and stay with her at night. Depending on how things go after the transplant, I may or may not be able to continue working part-time. We have plenty of offers of help from relatives and friends, but the closest description of my attitude is the loneliness of soldiers about to attack: fear, excitement, and the prayerful hope of survival.

It's hard to describe my attachment to Lucas except to say that he evokes a strength of feeling in me that is, as much as I love others, different from anything I have experienced before. Part of the completeness and un-alloyed quality of my love for him is the easy way he reciprocates affection. This ability continually amazes and delights me. Last night when he wanted me to tell him something, he promised me "a thousand hugs" if I would answer his question. His cuteness has always made him irresistible. His hair loss and anemic pale-ness convey a vulnerability that makes me want to hold him every time I see him. He is more like Andrew was as a child now that he has lost weight—so pliable and warm. Tonight he lay beside me on the couch watch-ing the Disney Channel. Now and then he would take a break to exercise on his new rowing machine, which makes him feel stronger every time he uses it.

And now I am preparing to reach back across the years with a literal infusion of my deepest self into his body. Everything else I have been or done shrinks to insignificance beside this act. If it succeeds, I think I will be able to face my own death, whenever it comes, with equanimity and a feeling of success. If it fails . . . I cannot bear the thought.

MARCH 2, 1992

A couple of quotes from a talk by Bernie Siegel, a guru of attitudinal healing, who was at Hopkins this evening:

I don't want to be saved; I want to be spent.

Fritz Perls

—

In the service of love there are only wounded soldiers.

We are now in the preliminaries before Lucas's admission to Hopkins next week. He and I have been examined and x-rayed, our hearts looked at, and loads of blood drawn. Our spirits are good, though this return to the hospital after a couple of weeks away has triggered some ominous questions, which he posed last night as we lay in bed:

"Can kids die of cancer?"

"Sometimes, Lukey, but not you."

"If they do," he then asked, "are they put in a little box?"

All the memories of Andrew's funeral came back. I find it hard not to weep at the thought of my little boy struggling with such terrible prospects, but he is, most of the time, in an energetic, fighting mood. So am I and so, I pray, is my bone marrow. Clare, as usual, is able to maintain her equanimity and optimism better than I. I choose not to burden her with my fears, which I know she shares and are natural but are, under these circumstances, excess emotional baggage. Not to speak of our deepest feelings in this way represents a change for us but is justified by a need to sustain our hope and determination and to transmit these attitudes to Lucas. To mobilize as many thoughts and as much prayer as possible, I wrote an op-ed piece for the *Baltimore Sun*. They entitled it "A Father's Plea: Pray That Our Son Will Make It."

My family and I need your help. Just before Christmas we discovered that our six-year-old son, Lucas, has leukemia. Since then our lives have been full of hospitals and chemotherapy and he is now in remission. His disease has an unfavorable cell-type: acute myelocytic. While there has been remarkable progress in the therapy of childhood leukemia, treatment is arduous and uncertain and the side-effects of the chemicals used are difficult to withstand. Against all probability he and I turn out to be a close, though not perfect, immunologic match—close enough that on March 19 I will be the donor for his bone marrow transplant.

The procedure involves an attempt to kill his diseased marrow with chemotherapy and replace it with mine. An experimental undertaking only a few years ago, this operation is now routine at major centers, though not without risk. It represents an attempt to cross the immune barrier, that fundamental biologic defense which distinguishes self from non-self. A major hazard is that the "graft" will not take, that his body will identify my marrow as foreign and reject it. Drugs are used to suppress this rejection. But in the weeks and months following the procedure he may be subject to a spectrum of complications including infection, bleeding, and liver damage.

As my wife and I have immersed ourselves in the literature of hope and attitudinal healing we have come to believe strongly that the combined good will and faith of all who care about Lucas can be a powerful curative force. We have received much comfort from those we know, all of whom are eager to do whatever they can. We have asked each of them for a photograph to display in Lucas's room so that he can see the faces of those who wish him well and are adding their prayers and hopes to our own.

One of the few benefits of this ordeal has been the chance to meet other families who are struggling with this awful illness. We are members of a club none of us chose to join and we welcome all the support and good wishes we can get, especially prayers for the recovery of our children. This is how you can help.

March nineteenth, the transplant date, is his mother's and my wedding anniversary. We take this to be a good omen. It is also the Catholic Feast of St. Joseph, Christ's father on earth, which we believe to be a very auspicious coincidence. Donating my marrow is the closest I will ever come to the direct experience of giving new life; everything else I have done pales in comparison. And March 20 is the first day of Spring.

I lie with Lucas as he falls asleep, and I look at the remnants of his beautiful blond hair, now nearly gone from the chemotherapy. I feel his breath on my face and wonder at the fragility of our most precious earthly connections. At these times he asks me questions, some existential ("Can kids die from cancer?"), some theological ("Can God hold the sun in his hand?"), some ordinary ("What does a dogfish look like?"). I find myself trying to explain many things that I do not know for certain and I have fallen back on the Quaker idea of God residing in everyone. He seems comforted by this.

During his trips to Johns Hopkins for treatment, Lucas often asks to stop by the old main entrance to visit Stein's thirteen-foot-high marble sculpture of Christ. It is a remarkable sight, my little boy gazing up at the great statue, drawing strength from the silent eloquence of that beatific face.

We now commit our son and our future to the care of those we believe offer him the best chance for life. We reserve to ourselves the healing forces of love and hope and a shared conviction with Robert Fulghum:

> I believe that imagination is stronger than
> knowledge—

That myth is more potent than history.
I believe that dreams are more powerful than
  facts—
That hope always triumphs over experience—
That laughter is the only cure for grief.
And I believe that love is stronger than death.

Please remember us to your God.

MARCH 5, 1992

Today I went in to the oncology clinic to sign permission forms for the transplant. It was hard to contemplate all the grievous side effects. Somehow I
thought that not having total body irradiation bypassed
the likelihood of sterility. I was wrong. The doctor, a
cool stranger, suggested a high probability of this occurring with the chemotherapy Lucas faces, though
some survivors are reported to have had children. I
find this devastating to contemplate since I refuse to
think about any possibility that he won't survive. His
not being able to father a child is a high price to pay.
Only with his life at stake could I accept such a risk.
On the way home in the car, I was in tears thinking
about the unfairness of such an outcome. Clare believes simply that he will be an exception. So must I.

MARCH 7, 1992

Lucas has been out of the hospital—apparently
healthy—for more than a month. He has been playful,
happy, attending school. And now, in two days, we
must take him back to be made ill again—first with
the brutal chemotherapy regimen to kill his bone marrow, then with the transplant and its possible compli-

cations. What if he's already cured? It seems unlikely, but his bone marrow taken on February 21 and March 3 looked normal. We must accept on faith that the chances of relapse are high and that a transplant after a second remission has a poorer outcome than after a first. And so we are on a train heading toward the procedure and the awful risk of graft versus host disease (GVHD) as a result. The symbolism of the father-son infusion of new life is compelling and agrees with the probability-of-cure calculations of the oncologists. So we will override our fears as we try our best to bring Lucas with us on this journey to survival. It *must* succeed. The doctors have cautioned me against accepting responsibility for the outcome just because it is my marrow, but how can I not?

If I have felt perfect love in my life it has been for this little boy. To fail at saving him now is a prospect beyond any comprehension or comfort. I thought I would feel less helpless at this chance to do something, but the waiting afterward is going to be awful and full of the dreaded free-fall feelings of powerlessness. Everything we do now has the sound of a clock ticking in the background.

MARCH 9, 1992

When we went in today for Lucas's admission blood work, a check by the dental consultant disclosed several areas of decay that could become abscessed while he is without white cells to fight infection. The result is a one-week postponement of the transplant. He will go in tomorrow for the tooth extractions under general anesthesia.

While this throws all the anniversary and St. Joseph symbolism out, the delay is obviously necessary and feels something like a reprieve. We're eager to get on to a curative procedure, yet reluctant to end this period when he is feeling good. We tell ourselves that God isn't going anywhere and prayers don't come with an expiration date.

From a card by Susan Nicolay, Center Sandwich, New Hampshire:

> The meaning
> lies
> not in knowing
> but
> in believing;
> not in understanding,
> but in having faith.

MARCH 10, 1992

Lucas underwent two hours of dental surgery today. This included eight extractions of baby teeth and a couple of fillings. He requires a week to heal before chemo can be started. He was, as usual, heroic about it all—not even a tear—and only one bad moment when the anesthesiologist was about to put him to sleep and asked him to "count back from one hundred." Lucas gave me a look of horror and said, "I can't do it!"—as if the entire procedure might have to be canceled. He then started from one and was asleep by the time he reached five.

MARCH 14, 1992

It is the Saturday before the Tuesday of Lucas's admission. I feel ready, I suppose, but it is so hard, seeing him full of energy and playfulness, to consign him to the torture and uncertainty of the treatment on which his life depends. I cannot believe that my love for him is not engraved in some way upon the cells I will give. I have the image of our lymphocytes recognizing each other with delight and uniting to destroy whatever malignancy remains hidden within him. *Please, God, let it be so.*

CHAPTER TWO

the ordeal

Children are the great gamble. From the
moment they are born, our helplessness
increases. Instead of being ours to mould
and shape after our best knowledge and
endeavour, they are themselves. From
their birth they are the centre of our lives,
and the dangerous edge of existence.

Their health, a random good fortune at
best, is often regarded by us as the result
of breeding and care. Their illnesses, when
serious, destroy happiness. When they
recover, we live for years with the knowledge of what their death could mean to us.
The arbitrary nature of our passion for
children, who reveal so little of themselves
during their short stay with us, is, for
many, life's great romance.

Josephine Hart
Damage

Today we began the transplant process with the placement in Lucas's chest of the Hickman catheter through which he will receive my marrow. As he has with everything so far, he tolerated the operation bravely and was in good spirits when I left him and Clare this evening. Emily, Clare, his aunt Julie, and his sister Nina covered the walls of his room with posters of animals, movies, butterflies, and faraway places. There was a moment tonight that I will always remember: Lucas and Emily lying close together in his bed watching TV. I feel more confident than ever that he will emerge from that room on a warm April day, free of the leukemia that has so terrified us. I only hope that the purgatory through which he must first pass will not be awful for him. Ten days to go.

MARCH 21, 1992

Lucas is now in day four of his hospitalization. He has tolerated the first chemotherapeutic agent, Busulfan, well, swallowing the large capsules every six hours with only a little nausea. Tomorrow he starts on the Cytoxan—the name conveys its lethality. He's likely to have diarrhea with it, and the next few days promise to be hard. Tonight, on the way home, the probability that it will make him sterile hit me again. With Nina and Emily in the car I could only weep silently, but later I sat outside and cried in a way that I cannot recall doing as an adult. I am undone by the unfairness of having to inflict this awful penalty on our trusting little boy; only saving his life could justify such a sacrifice. I've got to get my anger and frustra-

tion under control so that I can play my part in this
rescue.

MARCH 22, 1992

Today Lucas started the IV Cytoxan. He is tolerat-
ing it so far without much in the way of side effects. In
fact, he has been so happy and active that I have to remind myself that we are in the process of killing his
bone marrow. He will be vulnerable to infection with
his immune system destroyed, even while we wait for
my marrow to take after the transplant on Friday. If
only we can get him through this process without the
multitude of awful possible reactions: mouth sores, in-
fections, and, most terrifying, graft versus host disease. He asked me tonight about going to a baseball
game. How I wish we were there now, all of us, in the
new Orioles ballpark, with him smiling and excited.
We all hang suspended between life and death. *God, let
him be through this and on to the rest of his life—please. As
you sacrificed your son, do not make me surrender mine.*

MARCH 24, 1992

And now we are nearly down to it. Lucas gets his
last Cytoxan dose tomorrow morning. He remains
in good spirits, with only sporadic nausea. The real
testing point comes one to two weeks after the transplant when we begin to see the first signs of GVHD.
I feel what may turn out to be a foolish calm about
all this. Lucas is about to be without his immune system, with the threat of infection that that implies.
On Friday I will play my role and then we are all in
the hands of Bob Norton and God. The *Sun* op-ed

piece has produced a great outpouring of good wishes and promises of prayers. Surely this is the best we can do. His room on ward 3 South is large and now covered with posters and photos—"another world" is what Bob called it. Emily, Nina, and I go in each morning and return home late. Clare is the preferred sleep-over companion. Without realizing it, Clare and I have begun, as many families do, to develop a sort of "division of labor" in caring for Lucas. She immediately took leave from her job as a psychiatric social worker and stays with Lucas virtually every moment he is in the hospital, most often sleeping with him in his bed. He seems to prefer that I be with him for procedures, perhaps because he knows that, as a doctor, I have been there before.

Lucas drew a picture of the four of us and I turned out to be the smallest. We had a good laugh about it, but the psychological sizing looked about right. Right now, though, I feel my life more valuable than ever.

MARCH 25, 1992

Lucas finished the Cytoxan today and started a variety of antibiotics as well as thalidomide, the infamous deformity-producing drug of the sixties, now reborn as an immunosuppressant/anti-GVHD agent. It's startling to see the multiplicity of tubes attached to the IV computers. With all this stuff being pumped into that little body, it's a wonder he's not getting more in the way of side effects. Tomorrow is a "day off" before the transplant on Friday. I feel an odd lassitude as I wait. I crave exercise, but it's as if I just want to put my body in a cocoon until they draw my marrow. I will spend tomorrow night in his room so I'll be ready for "the harvest" early Friday morning. I hope so much that the graft takes without a terrible reaction. I don't see how I could forgive myself if it doesn't work. It *has* to work.

(Day one.) The transplant took place yesterday. My part of it was uneventful. The anesthesiologist was unable to perform an epidural block and I remember him saying, "We're going to have to put him to sleep." Under the haze of the pre-op sedation, I wondered if I had stumbled into a veterinary clinic. I have some pain in the places in my hip where the marrow was withdrawn and a little difficulty walking. I was returned to a room just down the hall from Lucas to recuperate. He sent me a card, designed by Nina, featuring a Polaroid picture of my marrow infusing into him through an IV tube. He wore his sweetest smile and underneath, in his inimitable printing, he wrote, "Get well soon." With the worst ahead of us, I can only pray that I have provided him a new chance at life; I would gladly give him my own.

Three days after the transplant now with no complications evident, for Lucas at least. Both Nina and I have developed fevers, with headaches and lethargy. My temperature tonight went to 102.3, so I can't even visit the hospital for fear of giving my infection to Lucas. Each day without complications seems a miracle and our spirits rise. His blood counts are dropping dramatically; fever and mouth sores are supposed to be next. We are daring to hope that he will surprise everyone and get through this easily. The first seven to fourteen days after the transplant are supposed to be the time for the first signs of GVHD. He remains energetic: he rides his Big Wheel around the ward for exercise and Clare and Emily have stayed healthy to sustain him. I can't imagine why I continue to have a fever. Maybe I can have all the complications for him. I imagine my marrow taking root at the center of his being and beginning to manufacture the cells that will be his new immune system. His counts apparently don't begin rising until week three, so there may be rough spots ahead. Good wishes from others, known and unknown, continue to pour in. His room is a remarkable, healing place with dozens of pictures of well-wishers covering an entire wall.

I think that now I may be ready to grow old without the fear and regret that I always anticipated. My gift to Lucas, if successful, will give me a permanent sense of accomplishment, one that exceeds anything else I might have done or could ever do.

APRIL 1, 1992

Since my fever has persisted, I haven't been able to visit Lucas, who is going through some terrible fevers of his own—up to 105.5 degrees. It's awful not being able to be with him when he's sick. At least Clare and Emily are okay. We've just got to buy him time for the marrow to take.

APRIL 2, 1992

(Day six.) Finally I am better and can visit. My vision of my life has narrowed to a small tunnel through which I can see Lucas and my family and not much else. He struggles with impossibly high fevers but still tries to be a good patient—clean-catch urines, medicines, mouth care. We watch the oncologists closely on rounds, trying to read their faces for signs of optimism or concern. They don't seem worried at the moment, even though they haven't identified or successfully treated the source of infection. It is the most agonizing experience of my life watching him suffer and not being able to do anything other than sponge him off and reassure him. He seems to hear everything, though at times he appears unconscious. Clare continues to function somehow on almost no sleep. She daily shows reserves of strength that I find breathtaking. Tomorrow is the one-week anniversary of the transplant. They say his marrow may start functioning soon. He also stands a good chance of showing acute GVHD. How much can that little body stand?

APRIL 5, 1992

Friday brought what I hope is the low point for us. Lucas looked terrible: puffy, feverish with temperatures regularly over 104, delirious much of the time, a rash covering his whole body. The first reading by the doctors was that this indicated GVHD. He was so out of it I was afraid he was dying and, while the nurse changed his bed, I just held him in my arms on the cot in his room and wept. Then the fever remitted and he looks a lot better. The rash also started to appear more drug-related to the staff and they seemed to relax, so our good spirits returned. Clare maintained her equanimity, at least outwardly, though Emily was more like me: terrified. By the end of the day the crisis had passed. It was the burning feel of his skin and the sense of him having no immune system to protect him from infection that brought me to the edge of panic. I spent that night at the hospital, sleeping in a chair. Yesterday he had a lot of diarrhea, but his temperature stayed down and he was a bit more alert. When his mind drifts, it does so in the sweetest, six-year-old way. He says things like "lollipops" and "Miss Piggy," and sometimes breaks into a little smile when asleep. Emily was talking to him while "Wheel of Fortune" was on the TV and, after one puzzle, he said softly, as he often does at home, "Dad got it." Sometimes, when awake, he bursts into tears and says, "I want to go home!" When we explain the need to be in the hospital a while longer, he asks, "Can I go home just to visit?"

This morning Clare called to say that his diarrhea stopped about 1:00 A.M. *and* that his white blood cell count this morning was 134! This is far below normal but is the first indication that my marrow has taken and is starting to function. At a white blood count of 1000 they begin to think of discharge, so we are on our way.

APRIL 6, 1992

(Day nine.) He looks so much like a baby these days in his helplessness, with his hair nearly gone. The way he cuddles with me or Emily when his bed is being changed also reminds me of those wonderful pictures of him being held soon after he was born.

I remember that five weeks before Lucas was scheduled to arrive, Clare went into premature labor. With

the OBs and radiologists we anxiously looked at sonograms, which showed him to be of a size to do well if
he was delivered then, even while the dates suggested
that he might have respiratory problems. The labor
ceased and he was born at full term. He weighed ten
pounds at birth so the sonograms had been right.
Clare's sister Julie and I were with her when he arrived and we were all, including the delivery room
staff, amazed at his size. He was the largest child in the
nursery. I remember him as beautiful from the beginning, though his first picture does little to confirm
that. Because Clare had "rooming in," he stayed with
her all the time. I had a confrontation with the head
nurse on the ward when I broke hospital rules by
bringing Emily, then five, to visit him surreptitiously. I
remember the nurse's angry comment, "You're a doctor, you should know better!" As if he weren't going
home with us anyway in three days.

Clare and I have "incompatible" blood types and
there was anxiety about Lucas's neonatal jaundice or
yellowed skin. I called experts on this phenomenon in
various parts of the country and finally refused our pediatrician's advice to rehospitalize him for "photother-
apy," which would require that he be blindfolded and
spend time under bright lights to lower the level of the
chemical causing the jaundice. We couldn't stand the
thought of his going through that; instead we placed
him naked in his wicker bassinet and sat with him for
hours in the warm September sun. It worked.

My memories of his babyhood are clouded now, as
happens when things go well and are expected to continue. What I recall most is his constant and welcome

presence. He slept in our bed between Clare and me. Initially, this made his nighttime breast feeding easier, but it also bonded *me* to him from the beginning in a way unlike anything I had experienced with my other children. Periodically, Clare and I would talk, first to each other and finally to him, about the need to sleep in his own bed. He never wanted to and, truth to tell, we never wished it either. This resulted in a strange nocturnal schedule. He seldom slept before 11:00 or 12:00 at night, and it was fortunate later that we were able to arrange afternoon classes in nursery school and kindergarten.

APRIL 7, 1992

I didn't go in today because I had a runny nose. I went to church by myself and prayed with a sincerity I can recall only from my youth when last I truly believed.

Am I asking for a miracle here, the life of my son, and, if so, what right do I have to ask it? In a world full of unjust death and misery, what makes the life of this little boy so uniquely valuable? Part of the reason is selfish, of course. So much of my happiness is wrapped up in my vision of him growing up, becoming ever more extraordinary. The way he has dealt with this awful illness and its treatment—the courage and elemental goodness that he exudes—has struck everyone who has cared for him as exceptional. All seem reasons why God would wish to preserve this child and allow him to take this experience into his life and make of it something of value to others. There has to be some meaning to this ordeal, and I can see none if he is forever a little boy who died when he was six.

Our hopes rise as it appears that he is experiencing only a mild form of GVHD; most of the initial rash was apparently drug-induced. The graft has also clearly taken and his white blood cell count yesterday was 300. He is still feeling and acting weak and sick, but was able to walk the length of the ward holding Clare's hand and mine. Bob Norton is pleased. We are at day eleven with continued improvement in prospect. My notes from the day they recommended the transplant to us say, "3rd week: ret. to nl." Though we continue to be suspended between hope and despair, the pendulum is definitely swinging toward hope. They have started tapering his immunosuppressants.

APRIL 8, 1992

Lucas looked good and had no fever most of the day. He managed one lap around the ward this evening holding our hands. He also was able to watch parts of a couple of videotapes. I think I have started to believe fully in his recovery. In spite of pretenses to the contrary, my faith was really shaken by the high fevers and apparent GVHD last week. Now, though he is still weak and feels "sick," we look forward to the start of the third week in a couple of days because it will bring continuing improvement in his immune system and his ability to protect himself from infection. It was the knowledge that he was defenseless against the multitude of possible pathogens that has been so frightening. Seeing him lying there, looking so pale, with antibiotics running, not eating, enduring those awful temperature spikes, has been dreadful. The only comforting thought is the idea of my marrow taking hold inside him until it becomes his own, strong and protective. *God, make it happen.*

APRIL 12, 1992

It is Palm Sunday. From Mark's Gospel:
JESUS: My heart is ready to break with grief.
EVANGELIST: Then he went forward a little, threw himself on the ground, and prayed that, if it were possible, this hour might pass him by.
JESUS: Abba. Father, all things are possible to thee; take this cup away from me. Yet not what I will, but what thou wilt.

APRIL 19, 1992

(Day twenty-three.) Easter. The last ten nights I've stayed at the hospital with Clare to help with Lucas's intractable diarrhea. It has been an agonizing time with incredible ups and downs: fevers, blood pressure drops, rapid heartbeat, irregular breathing; times when he looked so sick I thought he might die in front of us. The rashes have been variable, and the inevitable drug side effects have made him look swollen and puffy. He has come to resemble his birth picture: no hair, face so swollen he looks like he's been beaten up. Through it all he has remained uncomplaining, only occasionally asking to go home. His white blood cell count has come up to 2,200 and they don't think he has an infection. Another skin biopsy from his back showed "mild GVHD" to go along with the graft versus host problem in his bowel. We anxiously watch his diarrhea volume. He is now at maximal levels of immunosuppressants and getting a course of seven treatments with "anti-thymocytic globulin," derived from, of all things, horse serum.

I thought I had been through some tough, fearful moments in my life, but they are as nothing compared with the horror of these nights. There are some losses that simply can't be contemplated. One encouraging moment came on a night when he was feverish and practically unconscious. One of the nurses, sensing our distress, looked at him and said, "He's just lying there healing." Over the last few days he has seemed clinically better, more alert and engaged, watching some TV. He's been able to do a couple of laps around the ward even though it's hard for him. I see him as recovering, however slowly; I just wish the diarrhea would stop. When it does, he should be ready for discharge. What a thought! Lucas at home, playing in his room, sleeping in our bed. *On this, the celebration of Christ's return from the dead, I ask you, O Lord, to give us back our son.*

The day before yesterday I was giving platelets for him to use, a two-hour procedure. Lying on the bed, a needle in each arm, I looked at the clock and noticed that it was three minutes past noon on Good Friday.

APRIL 21, 1992

(Day twenty-five.) How I long for the prosaic concerns of everyday life. I am just beginning to understand the meaning of chronic anxiety. The emotional ups and downs occasioned by the daily variations in Lucas's symptoms are a roller coaster in which we imagine we see an improving trend, as we must, since the alternative is too awful to contemplate. His liver functions are abnormal and it is hard not to panic. His diarrhea was down in volume yesterday but rose again today. Nightly, he spikes a fever that leads to blood cultures, chest films, and so on. Through it all Clare is better able to maintain her composure than I, in spite of the fact that she has been at the hospital continuously now for thirty-four days. I've spent the last ten to twelve nights there, but came home tonight to be with Emily and take her to school tomorrow. Today Lucas talked a lot about the places he wants to go when he gets out: Rehoboth Beach, Squam Lake, the Bahamas, a cruise, even "a hotel." How soon will it be before I can look at my son without an imminent fear for his life? Even the prospect of daily outpatient visits for one hundred days, or a surgical mask in public for six months, or a year away from school seems as nothing compared with this day-to-day oscillation between optimism and unspeakable dread.

APRIL 23, 1992

(Day twenty-seven.) The news is mixed. A biopsy of the lower bowel yesterday was equivocal but indicated the probability of continuing GVHD. His skin looks worse and itches a lot. His diarrhea has definitely decreased, good news.

We are beginning to understand this battle against GVHD as a sort of holding action: using the immunosuppressants to keep it in check until it "burns itself

out" while hoping not to be overwhelmed by "complications" (infection, liver disease) in the meantime.
Rick Jones, the attending oncologist now, seems
guarded in his attitude, and it is hard to sustain our determined optimism in the face of Lucas's recurrent
high fevers and general lassitude and discomfort. Just
when I feel the most scared, however, he rallies and
starts taking an interest in things like TV cartoons or
begins to talk about what he wants to do when he gets
out—go back to school, play with his friends. He is on
fluid restriction which, naturally, causes him to ask repeatedly for water.

Sustaining Emily's morale is another issue. When
Lucas is feverish or uncomfortable late in the day, I
can't bear to spend the night away from him, so I end
up taking Emily to stay at a friend's house. I know she
longs to spend time with her mom, but Lucas's need
for Clare's constant presence holds her captive. God,
I wish this nightmare were past and we could all be
healthy and together in one of the places that we love.

APRIL 26, 1992

(Day thirty.) Today marks the low point—so far.
On rounds this morning Rick Jones looked at Lucas's
rash, which now covers about 90 percent of his body,
and asked Clare and me to step outside. He wanted us
to know that he viewed the rash as likely GVHD and
regarded as "an unfavorable sign" the fact that it had
gotten worse in the face of the immunosuppressants.
He also said, "We've used all the guns in our arsenal."
His statements sounded tinged with hopelessness and I
found myself sweating and nauseated, near to collapse.

We gathered ourselves quickly and reassured each other about the uncertainty of diagnosing a rash and the need to give him time to heal.

They are increasing the steroids dramatically for three days in what seems a desperate attempt to control the GVHD. They are also adding an antibiotic to combat a positive blood culture. Lucas continues to be swollen with fluid. His diarrhea mercifully is less.

He was alert this morning and I lay with him and watched *The Ewok Adventure* on the Disney Channel. He may look worse to the doctors, but his spirit and ability to interact and look to the future give us all a lift. He again said that he wanted to visit Squam Lake. I wonder if a merciful God will grant us this modest but miraculous indulgence.

This dance with death, this forced contemplation of the unimaginable is wearing but endurable in the context of being able to be with Lucas, to love him and feel his love in return. There is pain in the unfairness of his having to go through this, but pleasure, privilege really, in helping him. My world has shrunk to the size of this hospital room; everything else exists somewhere in the realm of events that have nothing to do with me.

Nine hours later and our spirits are much improved. Lucas had a good day, itchy but alert. On the phone to his aunt Julie on her birthday, he even laughed a couple of times. His rash seems to be improving from the neck down, which the nurse says is characteristic of GVHD. He has no fever and the new antibiotic may have gotten to that infection in his blood. It definitely felt like a healing day. This is not,

repeat not, a dying child. The increase in the pred-
nisone may be helping, of course, but I just see him
getting better, talking about vacations, fishing, his aunt
Julie "eating popcorn off the floor." *Thank you, God, for
this day. Please give us more like it.*

APRIL 27, 1992

(Day thirty-one.) Today's rounds were more upbeat
with Dr. Jones commenting on the fact that Lucas's
skin and swelling looked better than yesterday. The big
difference is in his alertness and involvement with his
surroundings. Bob Norton came in earlier and gave us
a more somber assessment of Lucas's "severe" GVHD
and the "huge doses of immunosuppressants" necessary
to control it. We know this, and I likened our situation
to that of the early jet test pilots who got into inverted
spins. On the radio they didn't scream for their mothers, plead with God, or otherwise give up. They just
said, "I've tried this, I've tried that, what else can I
try?" We will never surrender, and we expect the doctors to support our optimism without needless warn-
ings that the situation is serious. We already know that.

APRIL 28, 1992

(Day thirty-two.) Lucas had a difficult night last
night with fever and chills—another low. This morning I was exhausted and slept through the two hours of
my platelet donation. Even though I supply only a frac-
tion of the blood products that he requires, we watch
closely for my numbered bag of platelets to appear in
his room. It serves as a small antidote to the helplessness I feel in the face of his body's awful reaction to my

bone marrow. Today, though, he rebounded, watched several tapes, played board games with his five-year-old cousin, Clare. Best of all, his rash showed continued signs of migration lower on his chest. He asked to see our home videos of last year's trip to Squam Lake. He longs to be there, as do we all. He also wonders "when I'll get my taste buds back." One of the drug side effects has been that nothing tastes the way it should, so that his nutrition has been entirely through the Hickman catheter since the transplant. He saw himself eating a hot dog on the tape and asked for one. I ran out to a street-corner vendor on Broadway, but when Lucas tasted it he couldn't eat it, just as he has been unable to eat any of his favorite foods: pizza, soft pretzels.

We are on a tightrope, working without a net. Our balance pole is the skill of the oncologists and their arsenal of drugs. If we can stay here long enough he will heal.

My prayers tend to be formless but earnest, usually simple pleas to God to spare the life of this blameless and amazing child. I've repeated the Lord's Prayer, with its emphasis on forgiveness, many times. Is there anyone I *haven't* yet forgiven? If so, I forgive them now.

APRIL 29, 1992

Today marks one year since Andrew took his life. *If you can, Andrew, help us.* Lucas had a 104-degree fever this morning and several episodes of diarrhea. I feel that if we can get to May, then we will have escaped this cruel month and arrived at a more propitious time for healing.

The rash continues to improve. His face has been transformed. A week ago he was puffy, he could barely open his eyes, and his ears were encrusted. Now he is wan but looks like his old self. I feel as though I am getting my little boy back one inch at a time as the rash recedes down his body. I imagine, too, that I see surprise and increased hope in the eyes of the oncologists. Rick Jones says that with the reduction of the immunosuppressants, we should get an idea within a week whether the acute GVHD will remain controllable. Another time to wait. His white count today was normal. At least he has that defense against infection. Now he and Emily are watching *The Neverending Story* together. His eyes are bright, his temperature is down, and it seems possible to glimpse a life beyond this hospital room in which we have been imprisoned for forty-two days.

This situation resembles combat in that it really can't be explained in all its horror, exhaustion, and anxiety to someone who hasn't experienced it. Also, there is no simple answer to the most often asked question from friends, "How's Lucas doing?" To say the truth, which is "He's still balanced on the tightrope, but could fall to his death at any moment, and no, there is nothing (short of a cure for GVHD) that you or anyone else can do to help right now," would be an unappreciative, though accurate, response to well-meaning expressions of concern.

The gestures that have made a difference are the contributions of vacation time from the people with whom I work. They have allowed me to stay here. How could I be anywhere else?

When something is too much desired, then super-
stition sets in and a search for omens begins. So I wish
for April to be over. I look at the flagpole atop a downtown building and take comfort if the flag is flying
in the wind. Irrational, of course, but I passed the
bounds of rational control some way back. I suppose
my continual praying is a similar phenomenon, though
I have achieved a beginning sense that I am speaking to
a caring force that may listen. There is comfort in this.

In the face of all these emotional fluctuations, I try
to follow Clare's lead in maintaining an outward sense
of equanimity and optimism. This allows us to function in caring for Lucas as well as providing support
for Emily, who still goes to school and visits each afternoon. Sometimes, when things are going badly, I
feel like I am, by concealing my worst fears, playing a
role. The alternative, however, to manifest openly
these oscillations between hope and despair, would
render us of little use to anyone.

MAY 1, 1992

Over the last day Lucas has had nearly unremitting
chills and fevers. We hope that the new antibiotic
started yesterday will get control of what is probably a
blood-borne infection. His body from the chest down
is still swollen, with blistering and skin sloughing, like a
bad burn. The GVHD team was noncommittal today,
offering only some skin-care suggestions. We are now
at day thirty-five and at least have made it into May.
The waiting, especially when he feels poorly, is hard.
What are we waiting for? His upper chest and arms are
clear, but so much of his body is covered by that angry

rash, and his feet are a mess of blisters and dead skin. If they cannot control the infection in his blood, they may have to replace his Hickman catheter. I hate to think of him getting general anesthesia in this condition.

After a difficult night and morning, he and Clare are sleeping side by side, with her wrapped in his IV lines. He breathes rapidly and makes small moaning noises. I always try to think of him healing in his sleep, at least getting some relief from the discomfort of what he calls "the shivers."

I have given up completely on trying to work. Nothing of particular value exists beyond this room. Any phone call seems like an intrusion. His white count remains normal but he requires daily transfusions. I give platelets twice a week and sleep through the two hours it takes to do so.

The thought that really tortures me is that these are my cells attacking Lucas's body so relentlessly. I knew that this was a possibility but never really believed that it would happen. Am I so in need of more lessons in humility and powerlessness?

The old mariners' prayer is my own: *Dear Lord, be good to me. Your sea is so wide and my boat is so small.*

MAY 3, 1992

Lucas seems to be improving slowly. We had a birthday party for Clare's sister Julie yesterday and Luke got upset at the gift giving. At first we thought it was because he wanted presents too, but it turned out that he felt bad about not having anything to give Julie. Such a priceless soul must be allowed at least another seventy years to enrich the world.

His fevers are better, the diarrhea has virtually stopped, and the oncologists are encouraged. Maybe in a couple of weeks we'll have him out of here.

The TV news provides a backdrop of the Rodney King verdict and the Los Angeles riots over the last few days. In a world so filled with inhumanity, the value of this amazing child's life is magnified.

Lucas and I have always had a special bond, but being together so much over the last few weeks has intensified these feelings. Often when I pull his covers up to his neck or kiss him on the head, he will open his eyes and say "I love you." He wants me here every night and I can't imagine leaving.

Twice a day I take him in my arms and step on the scale. Then I am weighed and the subtraction is done to get his weight. Right now he is twenty-two pounds above normal—all fluid in his abdomen and legs in response to the GVHD. We also bathe him once a day in a giant plastic tub in which he soaks to help heal his skin. The new antibiotic seems to be controlling his fevers, and his blood cultures have turned negative.

Last night we all watched videotapes of the Bahamas and Squam and a 1987 Easter egg hunt. We laughed at the happy scenes and took new hope that we could be like that again: healthy and together.

This disease has—temporarily, I pray—robbed him of his body. His face is round from the steroids. When the covers are turned down, his swollen abdomen and peeling legs and feet are frightful to look at. His arms and hands are much better. For a time he would just look at his puffy fingers with amazement and horror, though he has not complained or asked the obvious question, "What's happening to me?"

Tonight I feel close to despair. Lucas's face is swollen again, his eyes almost closed, his lips and ears crusted. More ominous, his legs are sloughing skin. His feet look blackened and gangrenous. He is also jaundiced and his lab studies show liver damage. The high-dose immunosuppressants are toxic to his kidneys. The doctors seem surprised that he is not leaking fluid into his lungs, though that will inevitably occur if the GVHD progresses. He is intruded upon constantly: by physical therapy, ophthalmology, bathing, ointment applications, weighing, vital signs, blood drawing. Through it all, he remains stoic and uncomplaining. It is impossible to give up hope when he remains so responsive, interested in tapes and TV, loving and brave. Clare is indomitably optimistic and I must be also. Emily is scared but tries not to show it or perhaps even admit it to herself. We all soldier on in the hope that catastrophe will not overtake him before this dreadful disease burns out.

We now have access to "The Hopkins Suite" donated by Chris and Debbie Smith, the owners of the Tremont Plaza hotel downtown. From the nineteenth-floor window Lucas's room is visible. Emily and Clare's sister Ann are spending nights there. The hotel staff is wonderfully attentive, and it provides a refuge from the unremitting strain of the hospital. When we finally get him out of here, we might all move into the Tremont during his required daily outpatient follow-up. Tonight, when he heard that Ann and Emily were there, he said, "I want to go to a hotel." Me too. How wonderful to imagine all of us together in that comfortable place.

(Day thirty-nine.) Another "corridor conference" called this morning by Rick Jones to verify that, if the worst happens and Lucas is overtaken by a lung infection, we will support their "aggressive" care plan of intubation and transfer to the Pediatric Intensive Care Unit. He said that he didn't anticipate this occurring, but at this high level of immunosuppressants, infection remains a dangerous threat. Rick characterized the treatment now as "a race" between complications and a remission in the GVHD. It's astonishing how much uncertainty we have come to tolerate. During a quiet moment this morning, I thought of the ego-obliterating aspects of this whole experience. Nothing in my life has been as important or as hard for me to influence as this struggle for Lucas's life. Just being here to help catch his urine, give him water, carry him to and from his bath, hold him while he's weighed is very little and more than enough. The whole meaning of this illness, indeed his entire life, has been to love him as much as we can for as long as we can. It is at once my obligation and deepest pleasure. Nothing else matters, so this is what we do.

At times it is impossible not to wonder what any of us could have done to deserve this. Not a rational thought, to be sure, but inevitable. Has my life been too easy, my happiness too complete, my faith too weak, my pride too manifest? I struggle with the seemingly contradictory concepts of random misfortune and a just, all-seeing power in the universe. At the core of my confusion is my habitual preoccupation with meaning and the image of my child, his body swollen with fluid, his skin bruised and reddened, his grip on life become so fragile. What can this possibly mean? I suppose I simply am not enough of a believer to accept all this as the inexplicable will of God. Perhaps that, after all, is my failing, but, if so, why should my wholly innocent child have to suffer also? Whose sins is he redeeming? Who am I to ask?

When I donate platelets twice a week, they take my vital signs. It seems amazing and unfair that I am so routinely normal when we are continually looking at such awful temperatures with Lucas. As I encounter people off the ward, in the cafeteria, walking the street, I am again struck by their seeming unawareness of the gifts of health and an intact immune system that are so indiscriminately bestowed.

At evening rounds, Rick Jones said that acute GVHD normally "burns out" within sixty days. Can we hang on for another three weeks? It seems hardly a moment in a normal life; balanced on this tightrope over the abyss, it feels like an eternity.

MAY 6, 1992

(Day forty.) The nursing staff on this floor are amazing: competent, thorough, knowledgeable, compassionate. It may be that Lucas's fortitude in the face of all adversity is evoking a special response. Mostly they just seem like an extraordinary group of women.

The rhythm of these days: rounds, bath, skin care, vital signs, lab results, picking up Emily, bedpan runs, intermittent eating, hope, discouragement, terror. It's hard to maintain composure; Clare remains calm, but

I see my fear reflected in her eyes. It feels like we're on a runaway train.

Today is my son Michael's twenty-third birthday. I was thinking about the day I found him as an infant in an orphanage while I was in Vietnam, and another incident in the war came to mind:

I was serving as a medical officer at a field hospital near the town of Xuan Loc on Christmas Eve, 1968. We were suddenly overwhelmed with ambulances bringing in children who had been burned by the explosion of a white phosphorus grenade in a crowd celebrating the holiday. Several died of their wounds in front of me that night as I struggled to save them. Now my own son lies sick unto death, looking much as they did, and I feel across the years the same sense of helplessness in the face of an implacable, unjust fate.

I went to the war, among other things, to discover the meaning of courage. I never imagined that I'd finally learn it from a six-year-old boy, his sister, and his mother.

MAY 7, 1992

Lucas continues to have morning fever spikes. What is it? Infection? GVHD? No one is sure. He craves milk, which we ration to prevent diarrhea. He talks about pizza, the mall, watches cartoon tapes and the Disney Channel. It's so hard to remember us there at Disney World with Lucas healthy and running around, meeting his hero Mickey Mouse. It feels like we have been in this hospital forever; one day runs into the next, but toward what end?

As Lucas has gotten more swollen and unwieldy, the

twice-daily weighing ceremony has become increasingly important to me, and I think to him. When the nurse's aide brings the scale in the room, he looks at me and reaches out his arm to place it around my neck. I slide my arms carefully under his knees and shoulders, lift him, and step onto the scale. This is not a comfortable process for him with his tender skin, but he endures it uncomplainingly. We hope each time for a decrease toward his "ideal weight," and each tenth of a kilo in that direction is cause for rejoicing in the same way that every normal temperature is welcomed. As Clare and I changed his diaper tonight, he looked at me and said, "I love your voice. I love your face."

MAY 8, 1992

(Day forty-two.) Lucas's liver studies look worse. A sonogram is going to be done today to rule out gallstones, but if this is negative there appears to be nothing to do but watch and wait. His speech has become slurred, his breathing labored. He has a fever with chills and is very jaundiced. Is this the end? *Please, God, no.*

My mother, I have recently learned, suffers from Alzheimer's disease. This fate may be in my genes too, and I might at some point have to face the loss of my past. Perhaps by the time this happens I will welcome it. Some memories are too terrible for the heart to hold.

CHAPTER THREE

defeat

> Come away, O human child!
> To the waters and the wild
> With a faery, hand in hand,
> For the world's more full of weeping
> than you can understand.
>
> William Butler Yeats
> "The Stolen Child"

MAY 9, 1992

(Day forty-three.) Last night Lucas asked me to lie with him as he fitfully slept, often opening his eyes to look at me for reassurance, telling me a couple of times that he loved me, in his now nearly incomprehensible but beautiful voice. It reminds me that the only fear that he has manifested through all this has been that of being alone. As Clare was taking him to X ray last week, she stopped to give someone directions. Lucas immediately turned around as his stretcher moved away and cried, "Come with me, Mom, I need you."

Today the chronicle of horrors continues. For reasons that aren't clear, Lucas has slipped into a nearly comatose state, though he's arousable.

A chest film this morning showed, according to the pulmonary consultant, a beginning indication of pneumonia. We were soon back in the operating room so they could look into his lungs with a bronchoscope. He was then transferred to the Pediatric Intensive Care Unit (PICU), which most resembles a physiology laboratory. His rapid respiration persists and he is less responsive than ever, hardly able to ask for water. Now, in the sterile PICU environment, hooked up to monitors and IVs, he looks terrible: yellow, breathing fast, barely conscious. It is impossible not to be frightened by these changes, even though the doctors are talking about the possibility of getting him back to his regular room tomorrow. The whole situation feels like one of those "bad news, worse news" stories. At times I want to scream, "Give me back my son!" but nobody seems to believe that there's anything irreversible going on. And so we wait.

His heart rate is 155, his respirations 60, his temperature 102. How long can his little body stand this? We apply the skin cream and (with special permission) sit beside his bed to spend the night. What can tomorrow bring that will save us? Some treatable lung culture results? An endoscopic exploration of his bile ducts? *Please, God, let him live.*

MAY 10, 1992

Mother's Day in the PICU. There are some sights in life I had hoped to be spared. One of them is my son lying swollen and jaundiced with endotracheal and na-sogastric tubes in place, a respirator running, eyelids swollen with blood. This is the worst day of my life. If only I knew that tomorrow would not be worse yet. His mental status deteriorated until he was barely arousable and the doctors became worried about brain swelling. The tube in his stomach shows gastric bleeding, so he is now on frequent transfusions. He has had so many of these that I wonder, as I wipe it away, whose blood is this really? A CAT scan of his head was normal, which is about the total of good news today. His mental deterioration is presumably from his liver and kidney abnormalities. So we have a liver crisis, a kidney crisis, and a GI crisis; his lung problem is yet to be diagnosed but they are treating him for a viral infection. Can any human being survive such an assault? Clare remains optimistic and keeps me from going mad with fear. Emily and Clare's sister Charlotte join in the bedside presence of which he now seems mostly unaware, though he did open his eyes briefly this evening. He cannot speak because of the endotracheal tube. We talk to him, stroke him, reassure him. I hope some of it gets through. What I would not give to have that February bone-marrow-transplant-decision meeting to do over. I must not despair with the happiness of so many at stake, but I am so afraid.

MAY 11, 1992

(Day forty-five.) Another day of sights I never thought to see, words I never thought to hear. Lucas resumed bleeding from the stomach. The GI people endoscoped him and found diffuse bleeding, no single site that they could cauterize. He is now on nearly continuous transfusions. The kidney consultant has him connected to a hemodialysis machine, which he will need daily for a while to remove toxins such as ammonia and urea and, we hope, increase the capacity of his platelets to clot and stop the GI bleeding. The PICU doctors still seem to regard all these catastrophes as reversible, so we dare not abandon hope.

When I slept for a couple of hours this morning I was tortured by a dream of a healthy Lucas, at home wrestling in bed with me as we have so many times. It was agony to awaken to the knowledge of where we were and what was happening to him. Emily maintains her amazing capacity to hold his hand and reassure him, able with the eyes of love to absorb how awful he looks. Nina flew in today from medical school in Boston and is staying at the hotel with Emily.

The flag atop the Citibank building in downtown Baltimore, visible from our old room as well as the PICU, has been down for the last four days. I found out the name of the operations manager and called his office. As I tried to explain to his secretary why I wanted the flag back up, I began to cry. She was understanding and the flag flies once more.

MAY 12, 1992

It occurs to me that I write these words in anticipation of a happy outcome; I couldn't imagine ever reading them otherwise. Today was a "maintenance day," keeping up with the GI bleeding with innumerable transfusions, a three-hour dialysis to reduce his ammonia and potassium and take off fluid. The nasogastric tube returns fresh blood from his stomach continually. The PICU staff is competent and, to varying degrees, caring. We play classical music on his little tape player ("My first Sony" reads the label) propped next to his head. We provide skin care and whatever other help we can to the nurses. His cognitive level is uncertain, and morphine is liberally used for sedation and pain control. Yet he broke our hearts with a puzzled, beseeching look as we changed his bed. How can my son, bleeding from both ends of his GI tract, survive this? His temperature is okay, as is his blood pressure. If only the bleeding can stop.

MAY 13, 1992

(Day forty-seven.) I'm starting to lose hope. He now has increased fluid in the lungs for the first time and the oxygen level in his blood is declining. His child's body cannot possibly sustain much more. We are watching him slip away from us. There is no mechanism obvious to me for letting go. Prayer seems not to have availed me (though I continue to pray), and I imagine I see my own failing spirits reflected in the eyes of the PICU staff. What is the meaning of such an ordeal if we are to be finally defeated?

I haven't been able to share my worst fears with Clare, who certainly carries her own but maintains her optimism better than I. Chasing laboratory results and vital signs from moment to moment all day is hazardous to morale: ammonia, blood pressure, respirations, bilirubin, electrolytes, and on and on. Any improvement is predicated on stopping the bleeding. Right now they're barely keeping up with almost constant transfusions. The worst moments, even though they contain seeds of hope, are when he wakes up and gazes at us silently with God only knows what thoughts. We rush to put our faces close to his and reassure him, but it's difficult for me to keep my voice steady, sensing how scared and in pain he must be. Sedation is quickly available and I pray that he does not suffer as much as I fear he does. Other heartbreaking moments are when tears leak from his eyes. I wipe them away, barely containing my own.

There is a curious rhythm to this place. Lucas has his own nurse, who spends most of her twelve-hour shift trying to keep up with his IV needs. This mechanical atmosphere drains confidence from us all. He is removed now from any familiar surroundings and can no longer participate in the rituals of hope and healing that have sustained us over the last two months. Emily has adopted an attitude, which we encourage, of almost total denial ("Do you think he'll be back on 3 South by the end of the week?"). This allows her to function in a wonderfully maternal way while she's here and still go to school with little of the fear and foreboding that are my lot these days. They prefer that we leave his bedside at 11:00 P.M., and Clare and I have been sleeping in the family lounge one floor below the PICU. We leave instructions to call if he awakens and have come up several times to be with him until the sedatives take effect.

I am weary with numbers, uncertainty, and bad news. When Bob Norton reviewed Lucas's flow sheet this morning, he commented memorably, "Well, these lab values look better than yesterday. I'd say the prognosis is grim but not dismal." They support his breathing, keep up with his blood loss, and wait for things to "stabilize." I cannot fully confront the awful fear that we are, with all loving intent, torturing him to death.

MAY 14, 1992

Just at the moment when it seems impossible to stand any more crises, something else occurs and we deal with it. We cling to the scraps of good news: his clotting factors are marginally better, his ammonia is down. We try to minimize the bad: his blood oxygen is lower, his chest film may be worse, he now has a fever. It is hard to fall asleep for fear that I will dream of him, and it is hard to awaken and discover where we are. It took three liters of blood and a liter of platelets to maintain him yesterday, and the red drainage from his stomach tube persists. It is amazing how his little body can cope with these insults and keep going. As long as he hangs on, we must also.

I find myself thinking almost constantly now of the unspeakable consequences of his death. Even though I ache at the prospect of his not being in my life, the most painful thoughts are of all the things he will not experience and the awful fear of his spirit being somewhere without us. It sounds like I am giving up, I suppose, yet I cling to what seems an increasingly fragile hope that the bleeding will stop and we may yet save him. I also pray that he does not, in his intermittently lucid moments, feel alone. It's time to dialyze him again. *Lord, give us a miracle. It would be so easy for you.*

What I imagine I cannot bear seems to be drawing closer. I hope, but I also see, and I know there are limits to how long someone, even such a strong boy as Lucas, can survive on life support.

I feel old and defeated. What have I done, what have any of us done to deserve this? If there is no answer to this question, then what am I to make of such a randomly cruel universe?

MAY 15, 1992

(Day forty-nine.) This morning we were pulled out of bed at 6:15 A.M. by one of the doctors saying, "Lucas is doing poorly. His blood pressure has dropped; he's bleeding out and we can't keep up." We rushed to his bedside and he immediately stabilized. They gave him four units of blood and two units of platelets pushed through the IV. Bob Norton came in and delivered a very pessimistic assessment of both his GI and pulmonary status: "It's like someone slipping downhill. You grab them for a moment and then they slip further. Finally you lose your grip." We, of course, don't believe him. We think he's going to stop the bleeding today and start clearing his chest.

Today was one piece of bad news after another. The oncologists appear to have given up. ("We've done all we can.") The chief PICU doctor is prepared to keep up with the blood loss and continue the daily dialysis, but his pessimism is clear. For the first time Clare has given in to tears at the bedside. My attitude is one of determination/resignation. Unless the bleeding stops within the next day and gives his lungs a chance to clear, I don't see how he can make it.

Tonight he was alert for a bit, struggling and opening his eyes. As we tried to reassure him before the re-sedation, I wondered if my son was seeing me for the last time.

It's Saturday again, one week now in the PICU. I'm tired and frayed but seem possessed of a growing pro-tective numbness that enables me to appear confident for Clare and Emily. I'm afraid to show my fear lest it overcome me. Several times I have started to the bath-room to cry but have come back, frightened both of giving up and of not being able to stop the tears once started.

At midday I felt a burst of optimism. The blood re-turn from his stomach tube seemed to have slowed. His blood pressure was down a bit but stable. He re-quired only five units of packed cells today. He com-pleted a four-hour dialysis that took off about three liters of fluid. The oncologists came around looking, as usual, like funeral directors. When they asked me how I was doing, I told them I felt like I was on a burning airplane without a parachute.

It is difficult to describe the atmosphere of this place: the antiseptic smell, the constant beeping of monitors and IVs, the nurses rushing around. There are few sounds from the children and almost no cry-ing. As one of the nurses said, "If they're well enough to cry, they don't belong here." Nina continues telling Lucas her amazing stories of flying through the air with him over all the places he loves. We play classical music or Barbara's healing tapes. He's on a continuous morphine drip and seems comfortable. Our spirits rise with hope for this indomitable child. How wonderful it is, even for a moment, to imagine a life with Lucas beyond this fiery trial.

MAY 17, 1992

It's been a relatively quiet day. Lucas was dialyzed with a bit of instability in his blood pressure. Dr. Berkowitz gave us a cautious and still grim assessment. His chest film looks "about the same." We left the hospital briefly today to take Emily to the pediatrician for a persistent cough. It marked the first visit home for Clare in sixty days. Our spirits rise in the face of Lucas's apparent ability to shut down the bleeding. I know the doctors would regard any optimism at this point as unrealistic, but what else do we have to sustain us? They are planning to start a continuous filtration of the blood, which they hope will pull off fluid and keep his ammonia in check.

MAY 18, 1992

(Day fifty-two.) There has been a "catastrophic" complication: free air on the abdominal film indicating a bowel perforation. Surgical consultants decline to operate in the face of his multiple problems. Recommendation: "conservative medical management" with antibiotics for the inevitable abdominal infection. I am beyond discouragement.

4:00 P.M.—Dr. Berkowitz talked to us: the worst has happened. Lucas's ammonia level after dialysis was higher than before they started. This indicates irreversible liver failure and is incompatible with life.

Dr. Berkowitz said simply, "Lucas is going to die, probably within the next twelve to thirty-six hours, and we must now face the decision of how long to continue ventilator support." Clare and I weep, cling to each other, then make the phone calls to family. We kiss Lucas, who is by now surely beyond hearing, telling him how much we love him, hoping he does not feel alone.

What is it that keeps us going through this? The wonderfully sympathetic nephrologist, Marie Christensen, believes that further dialysis today would be useless in trying to keep up with his rising ammonia level and might precipitate a blood pressure crisis. She has scheduled one in the morning—more, I think, to give us the sense of doing *something* than with any real expectation of improvement. Emily's determination to help him heal has energized us. I suppose there is something beyond hope that, however futile, causes us to keep pulling him toward life. We are committed to seeing him through the night. If the dialysis tomorrow doesn't improve things, we face another decision.

Nina and Michael will arrive this evening; Kirsten, my oldest daughter, from California tomorrow. I can't imagine my life without Lucas. The failure of my attempt to give him my bone marrow is a weight I must now carry until I die. I was supposed to protect him, to save him, and I didn't. How can I forgive myself?

Clare and Emily clarified for me the correct response to the question of when we would stop the respirator and let Lucas go. Never. None of us could forgive ourselves such a decision, believing as we still do in miracles and the power of the body to heal.

There is no evidence that he is in any pain; in fact, at this high level of ammonia he appears deeply comatose. At Barbara's suggestion we are placing our hands over his liver, abdomen, and heart while asking him over and over to heal. It appears that we are hanging on to hope unrealistically, but we have the rest of our lives to grieve and it feels important not to give up before he does. It is also something we can do together and for each other.

It is strange to be carrying around this conviction, supported by the doctors, that Lucas is going to die, while at the same time functioning as if he were going to recover. There is a sort of disconnect between intellect and emotion that allows us to love rather than mourn him.

I do find myself desperately trying to remember the last time Lucas and I said "I love you" to each other. The answer may be in a previous entry, but I haven't the heart to look back. Will I ever be able to read these pages? Perhaps not, but writing it all down has helped me get through it and given the whole terrible experience some lasting form apart from my heart and memory. Lucas, Lucas, Lucas.

MAY 19, 1992

(Day fifty-three.) 3:00 A.M.—Surely this is the last night. We are staying with Lucas in shifts so he won't be alone. His latest ammonia is higher than ever. It is growing more difficult to support his blood pressure and he is on 100 percent oxygen. I hold his hand and feel spasmodic movements, probably spinal reflexes, but reminders of the many times we have squeezed each other's hand. I reminisce in his ear about all the good things I can remember doing with him: the bike rides, the trips, the jokes, the wrestling on the bed. I doubt he hears me now, but it is some comfort to recall how loved he was and how little I would do differently. Clare is with me and I have never felt closer to or more admiring of her. Together we will convey his matchless spirit to the other side.

4:15 A.M.—Lucas's extremities are growing cold because of the epinephrine necessary to maintain his blood pressure. His pupils are dilated but weakly reactive. I read him his last book—*Elmer and the Dragon*—and now feel ready at last to let him go. We agree to the staff's request not to resuscitate him if he has a cardiac arrest. The end now can't be far off. With all the IVs and arterial lines, they have thankfully left us one hand to hold on this last night.

8:00 A.M.—Today, I think, Lucas will die. His oxygen saturation is dropping and he is on maximum respirator support. Several family members are here and, in violation of the two-visitor rule, they let us all gather around. I look out the window and God seems to be mocking us with a beautiful spring day. People are coming and going in their lives as if this were not the saddest day in history. What is to become of us?

I am frightened that the terrible images of Lucas that have accumulated over the last few weeks will be indelibly engraved in my memory. Probably not. I think (and hope) that I will remember him as he is in his pictures: smiling, handsome, happy.

His pupils are now unreactive so that perhaps he is already gone. *Take his soul, O Lord, and give him the special place he deserves until I can join him. Do not let him be alone.*

10:00 A.M.—Everyone is here now, gathered around his bed: Emily, Julie, Charlotte, Kirsten, Michael, Nina (with her beautiful and endless stories). He looks peaceful, breathing rhythmically on the machine as his blood pressure slowly drops.

His epitaph came to me as I looked at the faces of his family: NEVER A CHILD MORE LOVED.

How could my bone marrow have done this to him? Jim Shields, our minister, came by. To his credit he did not try to extract some meaning, religious or otherwise, from this calamity. He just stayed with us awhile and let himself absorb the pain that fills the room. Emily clings to hope but, I think, realizes what is going to occur. As Clare said this morning, it's hard to know what to wish for.

With the decision not to take more extraordinary means to support Lucas's blood pressure, it is dwindling. I asked Dr. Davidson what would happen and she said that when the pressure becomes low enough the heart will begin to slow until it stops. And this is how my son will die. My most fervent prayer is that God will let my soul join his when my time comes. Even the chance of this will make my own death an act of hope.

3:30 P.M.—Lucas's blood pressure is now in the 40/30 range, but his heart rate is steady at 115. Emily is close by his side, holding his hand and reminiscing about good times. She has an inexhaustible supply of anecdotes, and other people contribute theirs. My fear is that she will become emotionally exhausted by this prolonged farewell. On the other hand, she feels that she is giving him something valuable in their last moments together.

5:30 P.M.—At 4:45 today Lucas died. I never imagined writing those words. How can it be true? His heart stopped just as Dr. Davidson had predicted, slowing rapidly when his blood pressure dropped below 30. It was a peaceful ending that hit us like a thunderclap in its finality. Emily was distraught, bursting from the room, running down the hall pursued by Clare and me. Somehow, after all the preparation, her denial was intact ("I thought he might get better"). She rallied as well as any of us. They removed all the tubes and prepared Lucas's body for us to hold one last time. It was so awful to see him like that, blue and swollen with fluid, skin cold to the touch. Emily clung to him a long time ("I love you, Lukey, I'm sorry"). Clare and I agreed to say no to an autopsy; his body had been through enough. In a dazed state we gathered our things and left to stay in the hotel downtown. We couldn't face the thought of going home. Can this really have happened? What sort of God would allow it?

11:45 P.M.—It is incomprehensible to me that Lucas is gone. I sit in the family suite on the nineteenth floor of the hotel looking out the window at the lights of the city. In the distance I can see the dome of the Johns Hopkins Hospital where the body of my little boy now lies. Emily has consoled us with her talk of what a wonderful life he had and how she believes that, wherever his spirit now resides, he continues to feel safe and happy. Then she has a moment's pause and wonders how he feels spending his first night

alone. This thought brings me to the edge of panic.
Tomorrow we choose a burial place. We also need to
work out a service of remembrance for Saturday.
What does this all mean and how can I ever be happy
again after such a loss? He gave up the earth that he
hardly knew and left us weeping for ourselves.

MAY 20, 1992

So begins the first day of our lives without Lucas. It
is, of course, another lovely spring day with the sun
filling the window of the suite and the city going about
its business. The numb and dazed feelings of last
evening have been replaced with an emptiness that, in
some form, will encompass the rest of my life. Now
we must go through the details of his funeral and burial in a spot where Clare and I can lie on either side
when our times come. We must also deal with those
who wish us well, but who can do little beyond offer
condolences.

Looking out the window, I can see, about a mile
away, the windows of Lucas's room on 3 South as well
as the PICU. Would that my vision were blurred. I
watch the setting sun move a horizontal shadow upward over the oncology building, until now it is the
only part of the Hopkins complex to be darkened.
Family and friends have cleaned out the room to which
we went with Lucas on March 18 with such high
hopes. Was that only two months ago? *Oh, Lukey, why
didn't we take you in our arms and run instead!*

Today Emily, Clare, and I went to Columbia and
picked out a lovely, shaded grave site for Lucas in the
churchyard. We were going to get one on each side for

Clare and me, but Emily insisted we get a block of four. We then went to the funeral home to pick out a casket. We chose one decorated with golden angels; Emily thought it looked comfortable. The funeral home agent injected some unintentional humor by writing a reminder to choose eight "pall bears." Lucas would have liked that.

In the distance I see a medevac helicopter landing on the roof of the Children's Center. At last we are all, including our son, free of that place.

Emily has spoken the most hopeful words: "I know that Andrew and Mickey [his grandmother] are taking care of Lucas. It's a relief that he's with people who love him." *Yes, please God, let it be so.*

MAY 21, 1992

We spent most of last evening planning the order of service for Saturday. I focused on this task, hymn and reading selection, as an antidote to my grief and anxiety. At times I fear that in losing Lucas I have lost the thing I was best at, loving him and being loved by him. Clare found the most wonderful way of reassuring Emily and me last night that Lucas had the perfect life, had been completely happy, even during most of his final illness. He died just at the point when things like school and relationships with other kids might have grown more difficult or complicated. Oh, how I wish he were here, though, to fill the void in my heart.

It is hard to move about in the world, to see happy people, healthy children. I feel so vulnerable to feelings of jealous bitterness.

We stopped by the funeral home to leave clothes for Lucas to be buried in: his Goofy slippers and Waldo shirt. I also left my St. Joseph statue to be placed in his casket. His spiritless body was in the basement, so close but so unreachable.

MAY 22, 1992

Today I guess we'll go home. It will be hard walking into that house with all his things there, but we must face it sometime. We also need to make final preparations for the funeral tomorrow. I'll be glad to have done with the view of Johns Hopkins Hospital out the window.

MAY 23, 1992

Today we buried Lucas. The sky was cloudless, the air warm and dry. There were hundreds of people at the old brick church; many sat outside under a tent and listened to the service. The prelude included organ music and concluded with Pachelbel on violin and cello. We sang our favorite hymns. The "Readings and Memories" section was wonderful; it included a song from Kirsten and Nina ("Breaths") and concluded with an astonishing and beautiful impromptu statement of love from Emily.

I wrote Lucas a letter, which I asked a friend, Paul Shoffeitt, who had baptized him, to read since I knew I could never get through it:

Dear Lucas,

Wherever your spirit is now, I'm not sure there's mail delivery, so I asked Paul to read this to you to explain what has happened to temporarily separate us. You knew about leukemia, that it was a serious disease that we had to try to treat so that we could all go on making each other happy in this world. When the doctors explained that your best chance was to get some of my bone marrow, I was glad because I thought that, since you and I were so close in every other way, my marrow would get along fine in your body and would help get rid of the leukemia.

For reasons not even the doctors know, after the transplant the drugs they were using as well as my cells affected certain parts of you like your skin and liver and kidneys. You fought hard to overcome these problems, took your medicines, and did everything you could to recover. Your mom and I and Emily stayed with you through all of it, trying to keep you comfortable and help you battle the disease that was making you so sick. Many people, some we didn't even know, wrote us and prayed for your recovery. I never saw anyone fight as hard as you did. You never gave up hope and we talked a lot about all the things you wanted to do when you got well. Everyone who took care of you said you were the bravest and best patient they had ever seen. Sometimes I know you felt terrible and some of the procedures were painful. Through it all we kept loving you and you kept loving us. I couldn't believe that you never got angry at the unfairness of all you had to go through. I know I got angry that this had happened to you. I still am. And sorry, Luke, I'm so sorry.

Finally the disease affected so many parts of your body that it overwhelmed you and you died. Practically your whole family, all the people who loved you most, were with you at the end, talking to you, holding on to you, loving you. We still love you and always will, even though it breaks our hearts not to be able to show it in the way we did when you were here, by touching, hugging, kissing you. We believe

defeat — 77

that you are in a safe place until, one by one, we can join you. I think I'll be the first to come and it makes me happy to think of being with you again. Until then, I hope you can see us and feel how much we miss you.

I don't understand why God chose to separate us now. There's a lot about his ways I don't understand but have to accept. You were like an angel placed in our care for a little while and I am proud to have been your father. It eases my pain that Emily is with us; her shining spirit is so like yours.

And now we're getting ready to put your body in a pretty place under a tulip poplar tree right next to the church. We do this so we can visit every Sunday or whenever we want to be especially close to all our wonderful memories of you. Meanwhile your spirit roams free and, I believe, watches over us. Already the sadness and anger we feel at your not being alive are changing to good thoughts about all you gave us in your short time on earth. So don't worry about our tears now. They'll turn to smiles after we've had time to heal ourselves, especially when we remember what a funny, happy little boy you were and what a joy it was to love you and be loved by you.

Good-bye, Lukey—for a little while.

Dad

We finished the service with "Amazing Grace" and carried Lucas to the grave site. The family recited the same Emily Dickinson poem with which we buried Andrew:

> Ample make this bed.
> Make this bed with awe;
> In it wait till judgment break
> Excellent and fair.

Be its mattress straight,
Be its pillow round;
Let no sunrise' yellow noise
Interrupt this ground.

I then committed his body to the earth and his spirit to eternity:

Now take back the soul of Lucas, your son and my own. He was with us only a little while. He brought us joy. We loved him well. Please, O God, hold him close. He has never slept alone.

Somehow we got through it, the ceremony that will have to substitute for the graduations, the wedding—all the passages I expected to see him through.

The question now is what to do next? Should we go to a friend's house in Wyoming after Emily is out of school? When do I go back to work? Can I ever listen sympathetically again to someone's troubles?

I feel like a marked man. What am I except a parent twice bereaved? I am just realizing how much of my identity was wrapped up in being Lucas's father. It's what I was best at and I foolishly assumed it was a permanent state. But if I no longer have that welcome task, then can I be happy as Clare's husband, Emily's father? I'm so afraid I won't be as good as I was with Lucas, who approved of me completely and saw none of my shortcomings. *Oh, Luke, why did we agree to that bone marrow transplant? Even if the leukemia had returned, we would have had you for another few precious months.*

In some way I know that time will do its work and memories will fade. I fear that most of all. It can't always be 9:45 on the night I buried my son. But if I am to forget the terrible images of the PICU, will it only be at the price of so many of the small but priceless recollections of Lucas? They seemed of little moment at the time—coming as they did in a seemingly endless stream—but they now compose all I will ever have of him. Are peace and a chance at happiness attained only by forgetting?

Julie told a story at the service today of taking Lucas outside when he got restless at Andrew's funeral. Lucas saw the bagpiper in his kilts warming up and later watched him play the recessional. After we drove to the graveyard, the piper again appeared. Lucas turned to Julie and asked, "Why is that man following us?"

MAY 24, 1992

Once the recommendation was made for the transplant, there was no reasonable way not to do it. Given the numbers they provided—60 percent chance of recurrence of the leukemia on chemotherapy versus 70 percent probability of survival with a successful transplant—how could we not go ahead? Bob Norton carefully explained the possible consequences of GVHD, then said they expected to be able to manage them all. I think all the time about that meeting in February, knowing I could have said no and trusted Lucas's body to heal itself with the help of the chemo alone. But such regrets lead nowhere. We did what the best, most experienced people suggested and I have to find some way to forgive myself and them for the decision. The terrible anxiety that accompanied his illness, and particularly the time in the PICU, is what tortures me now. I don't want to see anybody outside the family and hesitate to leave the house for fear I will. Memorial Day approaches. My sons have died in different wars.

Today I wrote thank-you letters to the twenty-five doctors in the Medical Group who have donated more than five hundred hours of vacation to me—the best gift that I can imagine.

What hurts the most is thoughts of all the things I assumed I'd teach Lucas as he grew: sports, academics, writing, values, flying, skiing, fishing, sailing, how to be a man in the world. Some of these things I can impart to Emily, some not. In the end I never even got to teach him to ride a two-wheeler. The basketball net I put up in the driveway last fall is adjustable in height down to seven feet so he could play. How can I ride my motor scooter without thinking of him sitting in front of me, a strap around both of us, him holding the mirrors with my chin resting on his helmet? Tomorrow I'll take the child seat off my bike. We spent so much time with him riding behind me, talking continually, pointing things out. I'm sorry now I told him not to ask me questions when I was pumping up a steep hill. He always had questions. I so loved to try to answer them.

This evening I went for a run in the rain to Lukey's grave. There were flowers on it and a letter to him left by Emily's classmate Samantha. My first reaction on being there was to weep. The tent was still up so I went over and sat in it for a while, listening to the rain and remembering. What I recalled most clearly was Lucas's laughter, especially the gales of it I could provoke by tickling him in bed. He loved to ask me to "fight" with him, and our rolling around always provoked memories of wrestling with my own father when I was small and he was still perfect in my eyes. The times in the hospital when Lucas would invite me into bed to watch *The Ewok Adventure* with him seem unbelievably precious now. When I returned to his grave under that low-hanging tulip poplar limb in bloom, I had a different experience. Not pleasurable exactly—though I was surprised to find myself smiling—but peaceful, with a trace of hope that I would be able to come back there often and feel something other than overwhelming loss. Then I ran the three miles home. Given that I hadn't run in two months, I was a little surprised that I could get there and back. From somewhere in my heart the melody to "Amazing Grace," played by a bagpiper, made the distance flow by.

MAY 25, 1992

Can we really grow used to life without him? Emily pointed out that it seems so long since he was around the house, and it has been: more than two months. The memories of the hospital seem to be fading for her, though they remain vivid and terrifying for me. I think the fact that I recorded them in this journal may be responsible for that. Emily thinks that tomorrow she may want to visit Lucas's grave. I do so want it to become a place of peace and hope for us and not just a scene of weeping and regret.

I can't even read the newspaper yet without becoming angry that in a world of so much that is common and evil, a nascent flame of true goodness has been extinguished.

It doesn't seem so long ago that I was living the perfect life: interesting work, the love of the woman I most admire, and six wonderful children—two generations of them. Then God reached out his hand and touched me.

We all visited Lucas's grave today, Memorial Day. As we got out of the car, Emily said, "Hey, I bet Lucas would like a flag. Why don't we just move one of these?" Our better instincts prevented us from desecrating some poor veteran's grave. There were few tears at the grave site, but later at home on the bed Clare and I just held each other and wept as we tried to think of a place to go on vacation. Every time I see something new, I want to show it to Lucas; if I see something familiar, it reminds me of him.

I don't think we can face Squam Lake this year without him. Maybe, after all, we should head for Wyoming in July. Everything there will be different. It's a part of the country none of us has ever seen. We'll take Kathryn, Emily's best friend, with us. It's so hard for Emily to be an only child; she has temporarily taken over Lucas's spot in our bed.

I plan to copy this journal and send it to Bob Norton, the transplant specialist. I hope he learns something from it—about what such an experience is like for the family of a dying child. It still bothers us that he left on a Hopkins junket to Saudi Arabia on the day before Lucas died. Since then, not a word have we heard from him. Two of Lucas's favorite nurses, Lori and Laura, and Marie Christensen, the nephrologist, came to the funeral. None of the oncologists, in whom we placed such trust, showed up. Can they not, as we must, mourn their mistakes?

The nights are the worst. Emily is still anxious and sleeping in our bed. Clare often feels faint. What has gone out of my life seems too great to comprehend. I just didn't realize how much of what I am was wrapped up in the effortless and endlessly pleasurable task of being Lucas's father. I so enjoyed all the changes he had gone through already that I couldn't wait to see the person he would become. Robbed now of this, I wonder what's left. Watching and loving Emily, of course, but in many ways her wonderful nature, even at age eleven, seems already formed. She is also moving so rapidly and successfully into the larger world that she needs us less and less.

A huge part of my future has been stolen from me. At times I wish it was me in that grave, selfish though that sounds. Instead it is my task to absorb this pain, be what help I can to Clare and Emily, and find a sustaining meaning to my life. A part of me does not want to go on. For I have seen things that no one should have to remember.

> You could tell it sometimes right out at the interment, right while somebody stood over the grave. The preacher would throw a piece of earth on the coffin, talking about dust to dust, and for some it was as if they'd been slapped, and they'd let out a yell. They'd fall to the ground, screaming, and their kinfolks would have to drag them up to their feet. . . . Later, they were the ones who did just fine.
>
> With others, it was as if the sound of that clod of earth was a voice calling to them, and they'd hear it and turn and then something inside them would climb down and lie beside their loved one inside the grave.

And after that, all of the light in their eyes would be gone. Other children, parents, even husbands or wives couldn't reach those people who'd climbed down into a grave after their heart.

Gwendolyn Parker

I can't let this happen to me.

MAY 27, 1992

Barbara Siddle Bolin came by today and brought a copy of her tribute to Lucas, read at the funeral:

In January Clare and Gordon asked me to meet with Lucas to do visualization as a part of a most extraordinary effort at healing. In my time with him I was privileged to know an amazing little boy who taught me that the depth of one's spirit is not dependent on age.

I found from the beginning that information gave Lucas great comfort. He made very deliberate decisions about how he would respond to whatever adversity he might encounter. It was as if he refused to react except from the very depth of himself. In this way it appeared that Lucas often remained free of the pain or fear of the immediate situation. Time and again he endured without complaint medical procedures that were painful. I was astounded at how he used the suggestions in the imagery tapes I prepared for him; he was so steadfast and determined. Even four days before his death his indomitable spirit was evident as he did his part to stop the horrific bleeding. His courage made it easy to believe in miracles.

These amazing qualities in Lucas were manifest not just because of who he was but also who his family was. Clare never left his side. Hers was the courage to love without reservation in the face of devastating possibilities. Gordon mobilized whole communities to pray and gave the bone marrow that was the best hope for a cure. Sisters, Kirsten and Nina, brother,

Michael, and his aunts Charlotte, Ann, and Julie frequently traveled long distances to be with him. And especially there was Emily. What a devoted sister! Her loving attention kept the playful-child part of the little boy from being lost in the technology of the vast hospital. On the afternoon of his death Emily stayed beside Lucas, reminding him of all their wonderful times together, filled with fun and laughter and favorite people and places. When Lucas went to be with the other angels, Emily helped him to make the trip on the wings of her beautiful stories.

In all these events you could feel God's presence. Such love makes us aware of the divine and enabled Lucas to feel the trust and confidence that sustained him. Tragically, there was no miraculous healing. His family did not escape the terror of his death. But love made a miracle. I saw it as did others: Lucas Livingston was so loved that in the midst of suffering and defeat his soul was at peace.

There is enormous grief at the death of such a beautiful child. Our world has lost a courageous and noble person. Our comfort lies in his indomitable spirit and in the knowledge that he will live in our hearts forever.

MAY 28, 1992

Will a sign of at least partial recovery be an increasing interval between thoughts of Lucas? Now I think about him almost every minute. The images of his long death still haunt me. Surely the passage of time will help. Where is God in all this? And where is my son, my precious son? Today I made love to Clare. This must be progress.

We picked out a monument, Vermont granite, to be adorned by an angel praying:

LUCAS SCOTT LIVINGSTON
September 17, 1985–May 19, 1992

Never A Child More Loved

CHAPTER FOUR

journey

But something had changed, or was changing. Everything always did, no matter how
much he loved what he had. The only redemption would be if all the tumbling and
rearrangement were to mean something.
But he was aware of no pattern. If there
were one great equality, one fine universal
balance that he could understand, then he
would know that there were others, and
that someday the curtain of the world
would lift onto a sunny springlike stillness
and reveal that nothing—nothing—had
been for naught, neither the suffering of
all the children, . . . nor love that ends in
death: nothing. He doubted that he would
have a hint of any greater purpose, and did
not ever expect to see the one instant of
unambiguous justice that legend said
would make the cloud wall gold.

Mark Helprin
Winter's Tale

I get up early, drive Emily to school, and try to get back to sleep. But I can't. The pictures in my mind of Lucas dying will give me no rest. How can I erase, or at least soften, these images and remember him as he was in health, his sweet face, happy smile? How could they have put him and us through those changes? I never felt warned about those possibilities in the dry words of the "informed consents." What is the process now other than waiting for time to pass? Should I try to get back to work next week? Would it help to travel far away or will I just miss him in a different place? I need some faith in God, but where was He when we needed him, when so many were praying on our behalf? I feel old, as if I have lived too long, seen too much, suffered beyond any hope of redemption. I am empty, barely capable of loving those who need me. My best hope for immortality lies in a churchyard. And the world goes on as if nothing has happened. I don't want to be a part of it.

I've got to figure out how to redirect these memories. I took Emily to a class party this afternoon at the home of one of her teachers. While the girls swam and the mothers chatted, I found a quiet spot overlooking a pond and woods. Thankfully, everyone left me alone. As usual, my mind filled with memories of Lucas in the hospital, enduring all those horrors—and us with him. Both Clare and Emily appear better able to focus on his happiness and the pleasure he gave us. I've got to learn how to do this if I am to get past this bitter place that in Lamentations is "the wormwood and the gall."

Tonight Clare told me that Amy, the four-year-old in the room next to Lucas who got a bone marrow transplant a week after he did, died yesterday. The entrance to the PICU should have carved over it "Relinquish all hope, ye who enter here."

I closed the door to Lucas's room today only to be confronted by his poster of Bugs Bunny and the legendary "That's All, Folks!"

I can't decide what to do next, particularly about getting back to work. Nothing draws me there or seems important, but maybe I better try it so I don't just brood. I also need to see my therapist from other times, Dr. McClary, and talk about what has and will become of me.

MAY 30, 1992

Lucas was brave, now I must be brave. I'm not quite sure what that means, but facing the loss and finding reasons to live seem the main tasks. The hole in my life left by his death is beyond filling. It is a void stretching into whatever future I have left. I cannot see a child on the street or boys playing soccer or teenagers hanging out at the mall without thinking of what was denied my wholly innocent son. The fact that he had a wonderful life for the six years he was ours is insufficient consolation. He deserved much more.

Emily has been sleeping on cushions at the foot of our bed. About midnight last night she suddenly awoke, walked into Lucas's room, lay down on his bed, and went back to sleep. She has no recollection of this today.

We have decided on a seven-day cruise to Bermuda in June for our grieving getaway. After watching a TV commercial in the hospital, Lucas said that he wanted to go on a cruise when he got better. How will it be without him?

This terrible thing has happened to me. My little boy, whom I loved more than life itself, is dead of a disease that came from my body. I cannot let this become the defining moment of my life. I have people who love and need me and I must somehow absorb this calamity and go on. I have borne burdens before and I can bear this one.

JUNE 1, 1992

Why do I and all these other people live on when my son cannot? I breathe, I eat, I can walk outside, smell the fragrance of spring, feel the warm breeze. All these simple blessings were, one by one, taken from Lucas.

Sometimes, when I feel tired and try to sleep, I suddenly sit upright, panicked at the thought of what he, and we, went through in that hospital. Only time can dim those images, but how can it happen when they keep lurching to the front of my mind?

Today Clare went to the funeral of Amy, the little girl who lived only one week longer than Lucas. What kind of world is this? I went to see Dr. McClary, gave him a copy of my hospital journal. I need help.

It's the middle of the night. No chance at sleep. Both Emily and Clare were crying tonight. I've always been able to forgive myself mistakes before, but this time is different; I don't know if I can and it scares me.

My involvement in Lucas's death and the slow, pro-
gressive way it occurred makes me frantic when I recall it. It's been only thirteen days and I suppose I may
be expecting too much, but I feel used up. What can
the future hold but more terrible surprises?

Clare doesn't want me to be angry at Bob Norton,
but he's the person I see as recommending the transplant, then leaving us at the end. I'm mad enough at
myself; he's entitled to some of it. I sent him a copy of
my journal today with the following cover letter:

Dear Bob,

I wanted you to know that we believe that you and
the rest of the oncology staff did everything you
could to save Lucas. I also think that, for all your col-
lective experience, the ordeal that a family of a dying
child goes through is not fully understood, even by
those like you who have seen it many times. I hope
you will read the enclosed journal that I kept during
Lucas's illness. I send it to you unedited; I have not
yet been able to read it and perhaps never shall. I
think you might find something in it that will help
you respond to the plight of other families who place
their precious children in your care and then must
cope with unimaginable disaster.

While I do not hold you responsible for what has
happened to us, I think you will understand why I am
sorry I ever met you.

Gordon

JUNE 2, 1992

I am not a tragic figure, nor will I become one. But
I do get anxious, frightened really. If this child can be
taken from me in such a hideous way, then what am I
to believe in, to hold on to? I have lost any purchase on

my life. The landmarks are familiar, as in a dream in which I move but to little purpose, not knowing what to expect next. And where is he, where is Lucas? I embraced him, kept him from harm, slept next to him. And then I had to watch him grow sick and die. And I could do nothing to save him. Nothing to protect Emily from the awful sights, nothing to deliver Clare from the collapse of her best hopes. What does it all mean? I pray that God will at least grant me the favor of being the next to die. I cannot mourn anyone else.

JUNE 3, 1992

For something to do I write letters of thanks for condolence messages and include an appeal for Lucas's memorial fund. He deserves more than a gravestone. That suite at the Tremont was a help to us and we would like to create a similar place for other families facing what we did.

My own good health rebukes me. The simple acts of eating and drinking seem unfair when he could do neither for so long.

It still seems inconceivable to me that he's not upstairs sleeping with Clare on this early summer morning. I should be getting ready to wake him up so he can watch a bit of TV before I drive him to school on the scooter. In my memory I take his helmet off, hand him his backpack from the basket. He puts it on, kisses me, and marches confidently toward the kindergarten door. How old will I be before I stop missing that?

Today Clare, Emily, and I went to Lucas's grave and

planted some bougainvillea that a friend had given us. The flowers left after the funeral were dying.

I took the child seat off my bike. I thought of the many miles that Lucas and I traveled together. He was almost too big for this; learning to ride a two-wheeler was next. Clare wondered how I could bear removing it. What I couldn't bear was seeing that empty seat every time I walked through the garage. What are we going to do with all his things?

Tomorrow I'm going to try to work for a couple of hours. Two weeks since he died. It seems both an instant and a lifetime. I'm reading *Closer to the Light,* accounts of near-death experiences in children. It's reassuring in the peace they seem to have experienced, but discouraging in the reminder that Lucas did not return. I transferred Lucas's college account balance to Emily.

It becomes clear that I must somehow emerge from this experience a better person or I will not have fulfilled my obligation to Lucas's memory. This grief must give way to some emotion of more lasting meaning. It is a waste of time to grope for rational explanations of what has happened, even worse to flagellate myself for decisions made out of love.

JUNE 4, 1992

In going through some of the sympathy cards we have received, I came across this by Bruce Springsteen:

> Well now on a summer night in a dusky room
> comes a little piece of the Lord's undying light
> crying like he swallowed the fiery moon
> in his mother's arms.
> It was all the beauty I could take

like the missing word to some
  prayer that I could never make.
In a world so hard and dirty, so
  fouled and confused
searching for a little bit of God's mercy
I found living proof.

Today I went to get my hair cut. The barber said,
"Where's your son today, in school?" At the bank the
assistant manager came over to ask how Lucas was.
Later I went for a bike ride, my first alone without the
child seat. I went by Lucas's grave and invited him to
join me. Perhaps he did.

I worked for three days this week, three to four
hours each day. I surprised myself with my ability to
focus, though thoughts of Lucas intruded frequently.
The worst moment came when a patient, at the end of
the session, asked how my son was doing. Doesn't anybody read the paper?

A friend sent me the following:

And a woman spoke, saying,
  Tell us of Pain.
And he said:
Your pain is the breaking of the shell
  that encloses your understanding.
Even as the stone of the fruit must break,
  that its heart may stand in the sun,
  so must you know pain.
And could you keep your heart in wonder
  at the daily miracles of your life,

> your pain would not seem less
> wondrous than your joy;
> And you would accept the seasons of your
> heart, even as you have always
> accepted the seasons that pass over
> your fields.
> And you would watch with serenity through
> the winters of your grief.
>
> Kahlil Gibran

Tonight I went with a friend to my first baseball game in the new Orioles stadium. I noticed as never before all the six- and seven-year-old boys at the ballpark. Lucas is now frozen forever at six-and-a-half in my mind and in my heart. As I grow older, will I try to picture him as he would be then? Will the passage of time give me some relief from the senseless and demeaning jealousy I feel toward all fathers of healthy sons? What I miss most are two things: the unalloyed admiration I received from him and the love that he evoked in me. Being his father was the thing I was best at; I find it paralyzingly hard to go on without it.

JUNE 7, 1992

The mornings are terrible. I awaken early and there is an instant's peace before I remember who I am and what has happened. Then comes the crushing realization that he is not here beside me and never will be again. My mind begins again to review the forks in the road we traveled to the place of his dying.

Clare and I went to church today for the first time since the funeral. It was a baptismal service. We cried through most of it.

Clare and Emily went to the elementary school and gave one of Lucas's books to each of his eighteen kindergarten classmates with a picture of him and an inscription: "To _____ from Lucas Livingston, a friend to remember."

When he was alive, Clare often referred to Lucas as an angel. He had this otherworldly goodness and happiness about him. As I think about him now, I think he was and is an angel who has temporarily dematerialized but who is with us still, loving us, watching over us, waiting for us to shed our earthly selves and join him. This is the most comforting belief I can conjure and returns some sense of order, meaning, and, above all, hope to his death.

From *Angel Letters* by Sophy Burnham:

> We come now to the end of these accounts, the fallen leaves drifting on the waters of our mind, the angels' letters that have come —and are gone as instantly— like whispers. Were they really there? How is it we have nothing now to show for them except a sense of grace, a fragile hope, the knowledge of our unity, and a sweet shiver passing over us, all because these letters, beckoning us to higher states, carry the signature of God?

JUNE 12, 1992

I took the day off from work today to prepare for the Bermuda cruise tomorrow. Inactivity accentuates my feelings of oldness. I trim my beard and remember that Michelle Kupiec, Lucas's teacher, said that his favorite songs were "My Father's Old Gray Whiskers" and "Baby Beluga."

I saw someone in a wheelchair the other day and it hit me that what I am feeling is similar to the experience of an athlete who finds himself suddenly and permanently injured, unable to do what he has spent his life training for. I can't be Lucas's father any longer and this loss is, in a selfish way, as hard to mourn as the knowledge of all that he will miss.

What will it be like on this cruise, my sad heart afloat?

JUNE 13, 1992

We're under way. The departure from New York Harbor was full of memories of our trip up here with Lucas two years ago: passing the Empire State Building and the World Trade Center. Clare was crying quietly and couldn't bear to look at the Statue of Liberty where Emily, Lucas, and I had climbed to the top on that rainy day. It weighs heavily upon us that he asked in the hospital to go on a cruise "after I get better." We promised him we would and now here we are without him. It doesn't help that there is an extra bed in our room.

JUNE 14, 1992

We plow the sea toward Bermuda, lugging our memories with us. I continue to read about angels, which I hope will contribute to the peaceful acceptance that I so long for. With all the metaphysical thought and reading his death has provoked in me, I wonder if Lucas died to save my soul.

It strikes me as ironic that I started this journal when I thought to tell the story of my experience in

Vietnam. Now in the course of a year, everything has changed. My oldest and youngest sons are gone and I am left grasping for some meaning in their deaths. Maybe I will find it the way I started, in the writing.

JUNE 15, 1992

Today we went to the Queen's Birthday parade in Hamilton. In the afternoon we rented scooters and traveled to a beach near St. George. While Clare, Emily, and Emily's friend Kathryn sunbathed, I walked through the nearby fort. I felt so alone, thought of the things I could be showing Lucas, wondered what would have been his reaction to the old swords, muskets, and uniforms, the dim, stone-lined passageways, even a "ghost of St. George" on display.

I realized tonight that Clare and Emily are the only ties holding me to the earth. Without them, I think I would try to follow Lucas. There are moments when I think of him that my longing for his touch and his smile is so intense that I wish I could will my heart to stop. I suppose that this feeling will lessen with time, but I'm not sure I want it to. I'm afraid that what will fade is the memory of what it felt like to love him.

JUNE 16, 1992

The realization that my grief, perhaps all grief, is essentially self-pity may allow me to find my way past it. What is needed, of course, is courage. I was everything to him that I could be, the best I have ever been. My task now is to transform those feelings into something that will sustain and nourish those lives still entrusted to me. Surely I am up to that, particularly since Clare and Emily are giving everything of themselves to help me.

As we looked out over the ocean today at Elbow Beach, it was impossible not to be struck with the similarities to the Bahamas: the palm fronds swaying against the sky, the clear, turquoise water. Lucas loved playing in the sand, running from the incoming waves. I never taught him to swim. There seemed plenty of time for that.

He didn't know much about me, either. As with my other children, I anticipated with pleasure gradually telling him what I had done and seen. It's hard to have that bit of immortality snatched away, the idea that he might tell *his* children about me. It was like that with Andrew's death too. One of his college professors wrote a condolence note mentioning how proud Andrew had been, when the class was studying Vietnam, to bring in something I had written about my time at war.

JUNE 17, 1992

Andrew's birthday. I remember our cruise on the *Rotterdam* seventeen years ago. My father took the kids and me at about this time of year. I recall one photo from that trip, a picture of Andrew at age seven, squatting on a Bermuda beach, looking at a shell, I think. He was so skinny and vulnerable. Another passenger on the ship who saw us in the swimming pool said, "Your kids look really happy." And so they did.

I'm old now, fifty-four in two weeks. I feel so much older since Lucas's death. I had lost my fear of aging, imagining that watching Lucas and Emily grow would pleasure the rest of my life. My other children are well on their ways as adults now and have little need of me. If I convince myself that reunion with Andrew and Lucas awaits, I can have no fear of death.

The loss of my sons has brought me to the edge of an abyss. I stare into it and see only darkness. I would fill it with faith, but whatever belief I had in a just universe has been undone. I, of all people, should have been aware of what a fantasy this notion was. God knows I have seen enough injustice and random death. But I guess I harbored an unconscious belief that the really terrible, life-decimating tragedies were reserved for others. Now I wonder about curses and stigmata.

I've always felt lucky because I've always been lucky. When this happens, at some point you start to feel that you deserve it, that you've somehow earned it. I don't feel lucky anymore.

I told Clare tonight that "I think about him all the time, don't you?" The answer, of course, was yes, and we both began to cry. I said something about being sure he was all right. She said, "I hope so. . . . I just want him back." I start to tell her how sorry I am, but she knows that and I can't even think the words without remembering Emily at his bedside when he died: "I'm so sorry, Luke. I'm so sorry." I don't see how I'm going to get past this.

JUNE 19, 1992

Sorrow is no longer the islands but the sea.

Nicholas Wolterstorff
Lament for a Son

It is the last night of the cruise and we near New York. It has been a good time for Emily, who appears to have lost herself playfully with her friend Kathryn. Clare and I have brought our grief with us; and as we did things, I know she was thinking as I was, "Wouldn't Lucas love this beach? How much fun it would be to show him this parade, all these boats, explore the ship with him, look out at the ocean." How long, I wonder, will everything we do be accompanied by such regret? The familiar things of home remind us of him; the new things we do underline the regret that he will never do them. The sight of a blond-headed little boy brings me near tears.

The ship as a metaphor for life has been much used and the reason is apparent. I feel as though, in my rush toward an unknown port, I have lost overboard two children who were the most compelling reasons and rewards for the journey. Andrew chose to abandon ship, but fate took Lucas in spite of our attempts to rescue him. The life preserver I threw, my bone marrow, sank and took him down with it. The ship sails on, destination as uncertain as ever, but my heart feels buried at sea.

I know I sound morose, but for the most part I'm not. I joke with Emily and Kathryn, read escapist novels, feel an undiminished closeness to Clare. I fear, though, some permanent loss of capacity for joy that I imagine will grow more subtle, less noticeable with time. Lucas died one month ago today.

I've thought a lot about courage lately. In my work I have come to believe it is the quality most important in healing psychic wounds. Much of my life has been devoted to trying to define its meaning and so conform my behavior. With the loss of my sons, I wonder now what is required of me to behave bravely and with dignity. Clare seems to be able to do this as I wish I could, without reflection or self-consciousness. She went through that terrible two months of his dying in an unflinchingly loving and steadfast way that I could only partially emulate. Now I want to pay tribute to their valor, hers and Emily's and Lucas's; I'm afraid I don't have the words.

> What happens when you let go, when your strength leaves you and you sink into darkness, when there's nothing that you or anyone else can do, no matter how desperate you are, no matter how you try? Perhaps it's then, when you have neither pride nor power, that you are saved, brought to an unimaginably great reward.

> Mark Helprin
> *A Soldier of the Great War*

JUNE 20, 1992

Today, the return. I rode my bike—mindful again of its terrible lightness on the hills—out to visit with Lucas. I told him of our trip and my sadness that he had not been with us to marvel at the scents and colors, to ride behind me on the scooter in Bermuda, to sleep in our cabin on the great ship. I sat for a long time next to his still unmarked grave and wept for all I have lost. Then I took our familiar route home around the lake and past his school. In the tree outside the kindergarten room are hanging many hand-colored decorations, no doubt an end-of-school project. His should be among them.

It is summer now. Tomorrow is Father's Day.

Clare and I went to church today and again cried through most of the service. I am undone by the stained-glass image above the altar depicting Christ as a shepherd holding a lamb close to his heart while on his left, pressed against his leg, is a young sheep looking up. Last year I imagined Andrew as the lamb. Now he is the sheep and Lucas rests on Christ's arm. As the music and the words of the liturgy wash over me, I pray for some sign that Lucas is safe and happy and not alone. I doubt I will receive one, owing, I suppose, to lack of faith.

The pain is getting worse, not better. I can hardly contain it. Today I came upon a collection of his work and his report card, which his teacher, Michelle Kupiec, gave Clare. So many report cards have I seen, but this one ends "Your child's placement will be Grade ___." Her final comment: "6/92: Lucas was a joy and touched the lives of everyone."

Today I flew Emily in my plane up to New Haven and dropped her off to spend a few days with Nina. It was my first flight in nearly seven months, since our return from the Bahamas. Even then Lucas must have had leukemia, and us so happily unaware.

As I was flying back alone today, searching for something to feel good about, I began to think about the fact that Lucas at no point thought or, I believe, feared that he was going to die. Because we never believed it until he was unconscious near the end. Clare has spoken about how awful it would have been for him to relapse again and again until he got the clear sense that things were hopeless. I think he was spared that terrible foreboding and for that I am thankful.

What I feared most has happened. Lucas is now forever a six-year-old boy who died. We miss him now as he was and still would be were he with us. In a year he would have been so much different from the child we mourn. In five years we would hardly recognize him and will have only the memories of his angelic countenance smiling forever at us from his photographs—as he was and always now will be. So it's not just the grindstone of time that will dull our pain; it's his not keeping up with us or with the world that will finally, sadly, inevitably bring us some peace. That and the hope that we will see him again on the other side.

JUNE 24, 1992

I go through the motions of normal living. I'm working, bicycling, eating, sleeping, being with Clare. Sometimes I will, like any post-trauma sufferer, flash on images of Lucas in the PICU. I fight off panic and wrench myself back to the present. When I am doing something that we did often, like riding the scooter or bike, I can hardly believe that we will never do it together again. Over and over I can hear him saying, "I love you, Dad." I rode by his grave yesterday and told him how much I missed that.

JUNE 26, 1992

Sometimes it seems that the cracked vessel of my spirit can contain no more pain. Often this occurs as I am trying to fall asleep. The welling up of my grief threatens to overwhelm me and I am seized with the need to cry out. So that I do not awaken Clare, I go downstairs where I content myself with the low moans of a wounded animal until I can once more bring myself to return to the bed we shared so long with Lucas.

JUNE 27, 1992

Today, marked on the kitchen calendar for this date, is the circled number *100*. Thankfully, Clare has not asked me about it. In April, we were trying to make plans for the summer and I counted to the one-hundredth day after the transplant, the point when the intensive phase of his outpatient treatment would be complete. How long ago it seems since that flash of optimism. Three days until my birthday. When Clare and Emily ask me what I want, I can think of nothing except my little boy.

JULY 1, 1992

I was thinking this evening that I have always felt a wish that I could have another five minutes with my father to say good-bye. Not so with Lucas. He got everything I had to give from the day of his birth until the hour of his death. There was nothing left unsaid or undone. I treasured every moment with him and felt his unqualified love in return. Only this knowledge will allow me to heal.

JULY 4, 1992

Today Emily and I went for a glider ride; I had arranged it for her as a Christmas present. It was a beautiful day, scattered clouds at five thousand feet, the point at which we disconnected from the tow plane. We were up for about forty-five minutes, circling with only the sound of the wind. The pilot found a thermal updraft and we climbed a few hundred feet before settling gently back to earth. It was an experience to remember, the two of us squeezed tightly together in that small backseat, the Plexiglas canopy filled with clouds and sky.

None of us had much enthusiasm for going to the fireworks at the lake. I couldn't stand the thought of walking my bike up the hill without Lucas on the back. So we stayed home and felt the explosions rock the night.

JULY 9, 1992

Now we are on Cape Cod, at a friend's house. We flew up, with Clare alone in the backseat where Lucas always slept with his head in her lap. We had last been to Provincetown in August 1986, when he was a baby, flying down from New Hampshire for a day of whale watching. I walked a couple of miles on the beach last night, toward Wellfleet. I could almost feel the gentle grasp of Lucas's hand as I walked. I came upon a stone, worn to a smooth oval by the sea and spoke aloud, showing it to him before tossing it futilely into the dunes. It is growing possible now to think of living the rest of my life with this empty place in my heart. We laugh, eat, sleep, and do not speak of our missing child. I know that Clare, like me, thinks of him all the time, even as we make love.

We are in a large, airy house on a bluff overlooking Cape Cod Bay. The tides ebb and flow below us and,

amid all this history, I feel acutely the brief flash
that is my existence. Yet it seems important to find
some meaning beyond the pain and loss that is my por-
tion now.

The summer has a curiously misspent quality about
it. We had come to think of it as a summer of healing
for Lucas, with our activities organized around his
continuing need for care: frequent outpatient visits, a
surgical mask in public. Now our obligations to him
are over and we are free to go to all these places:
Bermuda, Cape Cod, Wyoming. The baggage I bear is
my grief and the frustrated desire to share all this with
him. I didn't realize how much I had come to see
everything through his eyes, enjoying his curiosity and
wonder; how it pleasured me to explain new things to
him. Emily already knows so much that I often feel I
have little to give her. When I talked to her today
about the tides, her knowledge was as great as mine.

The sun is setting off Long Point near Provincetown. It creates a highway of light on the quiet waters
of the bay. This view is one of countless such pleasures
I have had, but Lucas will not see it with living eyes. I
think his last earthly image was his father's face smiling
desperately, telling him that he was "going to be okay."
How can I be here, loving him still but unable to touch
him—or to share with him this sunset?

JULY 12, 1992

Let me suggest that the bad things that happen to us in
our lives do not have a meaning when they happen.
They do not occur for any good reason which would
cause us to accept them willingly. But we can give

them a meaning. We can redeem these tragedies from senselessness by imposing meaning on them. The question we should be asking is not, "Why did this happen to me? What did I do to deserve this?" That is really an unanswerable, pointless question. A better question would be "Now that this has happened to me, what am I going to do about it?"

Harold Kushner
When Bad Things Happen to Good People

Kushner's words have been as helpful as anything I've read in coming to terms with the unfairness of Lucas's death. I do not need God's forgiveness; I need my own.

People talk about having "a personal relationship with God." I don't think that's possible, at least for me. I think I can have relationships with the world God made and the people in it. If indeed "there is that of God in every man," then I suppose as one lives and interacts with others, one is relating to God. I believe that, having created the world and given humankind some moral direction, God has left us free to choose how to live and how to react to the things that befall us, not by the hand of God, but by fate and the natural laws of the earth. The most we can ask from Him is some help in marshaling our strength and courage. If the cards we are dealt are favorable—as they have been for most of my life—we are lucky and the game is a pleasure. When, instead, we confront tragedy and pain, we can flinch or be angry, but still we play on as best we can until we die.

JULY 25, 1992

Now we are in Wyoming at a friend's house on the

Snake River near Jackson. The Tetons rise abruptly from the high, flat valley like afterthoughts of the Creator. Snow is visible near the tops, a reminder of how harsh and long the winters must be here.

I've gotten back to *A Soldier of the Great War* by Mark Helprin, the book I was reading when Lucas died, and have found much of it speaking to my current feelings, particularly since the main character, Alessandro, loses both his father and his son:

> "Look at the clouds," Alessandro said. "They pass so gently and so quietly, but as if with such resolution. Someone once said they were rafts for souls."

JULY 29, 1992

Clare was moaning softly in her sleep this morning so I awakened her. She had been dreaming: We were late picking Lucas up at school. When we arrived, the fenced-in area in front of the kindergarten was filled with children, but look as we might, we could not find him. The dream left us both weeping for a long time, holding on to each other. This place, perhaps because of its beauty, has given us the chance to freely grieve together.

I rode a bike about three miles south on the dike along the river this morning. I saw an eagle airborne in the wind and ospreys fishing. I tried to visualize Lucas's soul riding on the passing clouds, but it's a poor substitute for his soft hand and sweet smile.

This afternoon Clare, Emily, and I are going white-water rafting. We are in the process of creating new memories—without Lucas—which will inevitably dim the old.

Alessandro talks about faith:

"Either you apprehend God, or you do not."

"Do you?"

"Yes, very strongly, but, at times, not. The older I get, and the more I see how life is arranged and with what certainty and predictability we move from stage to stage, the more I believe in God, the more I feel His presence, the more I am stunned by the power of His works. And yet, the older I become and the more I see of suffering and death, the less approachable is God, and the more it appears that He does not exist. Being very clever, He has beaten life into a great question that breaks the living and is answered only in death. . . . Sometimes I believe, and sometimes not."

"What accounts for the difference?"

"My strength, the clarity of my vision, the brokenness of my heart—only these."

AUGUST 1, 1992

We have returned home, recovered from the time change, and are ready to get on with our lives. This Tuesday we are to meet with the owners of the Tremont Plaza hotel to talk about arrangements to provide a suite there in Lucas's memory for families of children receiving bone marrow transplants. How can we be talking about a memorial? How could he have not seen Wyoming with us? He would have so loved that rodeo.

AUGUST 4, 1992

Though my grieving is undiminished, I seem to have less to say about it these days. Perhaps that's how it is with a permanent loss: you examine it from every angle you can think of and then just carry it like a weight. As with all burdens, I would wish this one to become lighter with time. Perhaps it will. It is the way of grief, I suppose, to create new memories and live in a time never inhabited by the lost loved one. When things—when I—change enough, perhaps the laceration in my heart will heal and calcify until I can bear it without the continual imminence of tears.

I remember asking Clare at times when I was playing with Lucas, "Is it possible to be too close to a child?" I didn't believe it was, of course, but now I wonder. There persists the irrational thought that since my love for Lucas was so great, I was somehow required, like Abraham, to choose between my son and God. Unlike Abraham, and because I would have chosen my son, I received no reprieve.

AUGUST 12, 1992

I can hardly bring myself to go to bed at night, and then only very late, so that I am constantly fighting fatigue during the day. When I close my eyes to sleep, images of Lucas rush in and overwhelm me with sadness and anxiety. The house is still full of him. Pictures at different ages smile at me with the innocent trust that I thought never to betray. In the basement are his playthings and the contents of that hospital room that witnessed the death of our best hopes. His still-made bed seems to await him. Beside it is his "old-fashioned phone," which he received with such delight last Christmas.

Today Emily and I mowed the grass on his grave; later she and Clare planted more flowers. When I used to think about growing old, I feared the prospect of infirmity and a diminished ability to think and act. I never thought to bury pieces of my heart while the rest of me lived on.

I find that pain, like love, can be augmented in the sharing. Clare, Emily, and I carry our grief both separately and together; there is plenty to go around. Sometimes it emerges when we are together, but generally we try to spare each other. We go about our lives, laugh when we can, and wonder when memories of Lucas will cease to occupy our every moment.

> In our sleep, Pain that cannot forget
> Falls drop by drop upon the Heart
> And in our Despair, against our Will
> Comes Wisdom through the awful grace
>   of God.
>
> Aeschylus

Tonight Clare and I went to a Compassionate Friends meeting. When my turn came to describe our loss, I just dissolved in tears.

I also find myself getting angry easily these days. Just beneath the anger is my bottomless sadness that the one person who loved me without reservation is gone. I tell myself that he could not indefinitely have believed I was perfect, but I miss that so.

I think often now of my own death, with something akin to anticipation. I worry irrationally that if I live too long he will not recognize me when I come.

If only I could feel his presence still, believe that he was near me in some form. I'm haunted by the fear that his death represented some failure of spirit or faith on my part. And now my inability to reconcile my loss represents a similar lack of belief.

SEPTEMBER 1, 1992

Clare and I have considered the possibility of another child. I suppose it is a natural, though futile, thought. Tonight she gently but decisively made it clear that she could not do this. She's right, of course, but my heart covets one more chance to be a father. I know I just need time to treasure what I have and relinquish the longing for what I have lost. Sometimes it feels to me like he dies again each day. Where is my relief? I feel only obligations and other people's needs for something I pretend to be.

SEPTEMBER 4, 1992

I worked a full week, the first since February. It helps me feel useful and provides some distraction, but in any idle moment I still experience the feeling of hopeless amputation that I expect to carry with me for the rest of my life.

I'm trying to make something out of all this pain that might give it some lasting meaning. But how do I do that? It seems not to be enough just to communicate it. Perhaps it's too soon to be uplifting; I certainly don't feel uplifted. I was thinking tonight that I wish I could feel the presence of God, who I want to believe is somehow with me through all this, but I can't. I don't think I need a burning bush or a voice from the sky, just a sense that I will be able to extract some purpose from my life that will balance the losses I have suffered. I had a little boy who loved Waldo and old-fashioned phones, who thought I had no flaws when it was he who was perfect. And now I move through my life feeling like an actor in a play I had no part in creating. I say my lines, fulfill my obligations, but what will it take to regain the capacity for joy, which redeems the struggle?

SEPTEMBER 9, 1992

Sleep continues to be a problem. The process of turning off the light and remembering what it felt like to have him there between us makes it impossible to stay in bed unless I'm exhausted, usually not before 1:00 or 2:00 in the morning.

We just received an album created by Michelle Kupiec, Lucas's kindergarten teacher. It contains photos of him in school, some of his writing, and drawings made for him by the other kids. It made me cry, of course, but something else is happening. He looked different to me in the pictures, a little strange, and I realize that I haven't seen him at all in nearly four months; for at least a month before that, he was changed by the drugs and his disease. Time is doing its work and my little boy is receding from me as I continue my journey and he grows smaller in the distance. *I will always love you, Luke, and my last breath will be made easier by the hope of joining you. It's all the breaths I must draw between now and then that worry me.*

SEPTEMBER 14, 1992

My life closed twice before its close;
It yet remains to see

If Immortality unveil
A third event to me,

So huge, so hopeless to conceive,
As these that twice befell.
Parting is all we know of heaven,
And all we need of hell.

Emily Dickinson

SEPTEMBER 15, 1992

What have I learned in the process, ever incomplete, of mourning my lost son? That one can bear the unbearable? That it is possible to extract hope from the residue of despair? I don't know what the lesson of this tragedy is. What I feel is that Lucas and I so loved each other that we will never be wholly parted. What I long for is a reunion with his brave and generous spirit. Of all my unanswered prayers, this one abides.

CHAPTER FIVE

what is lost in the giving?

Nothing can make up for the absence of someone whom we love. It would be wrong to try to find a substitute. We must simply hold out and see it through. That sounds very hard at first, but at the same time it is a great consolation. For the gap, as long as it remains unfilled, preserves the bond between us. It is nonsense to say that God fills the gap. God does not fill it, but on the contrary, God keeps it empty and so helps us to keep alive our former communion with one another, even at the cost of pain. The dearer and richer our memories, the more difficult the separation, but gratitude changes the pangs of memory into tranquil joy. The beauties of the past are born, not as a thorn in the flesh, but as a precious gift in themselves. We must take care not to wallow in our memories or hand ourselves over to them, just as we do not gaze all the time at a valuable

present, but only at special times and apart
from these keep it simply as a hidden treasure that is ours for certain. In this way the
past gives us lasting joy and strength.

Dietrich Bonhoeffer

SEPTEMBER 16, 1992

I think about giving in, stopping the struggle to
grieve, allowing myself to rest. If I embrace the losses
I have suffered, I imagine a place beyond pain and faith
where peace awaits like the narcotic cold of the arctic
night. To keep moving forward, knowing that I only
postpone final defeat, seems an act of futile conceit.

For what audience do I perform? Can I admit that
no one is watching, or must I create a consciousness
that cares how I live and die, love and lose, laugh and
weep? Can I believe the alternative—that the effort to
be happy for a moment is a soundless act in a universe
empty of meaning? My burden is that I am, in my foolish frailty, condemned to the hope that my suffering
will be redeemed and my love rewarded.

SEPTEMBER 17, 1992

*Happy birthday, Luke. I imagined this day when we were
in the hospital, thinking of you recovering at home, nearly
past the time when we could stop worrying about one part of
your sickness—all of us together in happiness and relief.*

Yesterday we celebrated Emily's birthday with Ann and lit-

tle Clare, who came from Atlanta to visit. Your mom gave
Emily several angels to add to her collection on the shelf in
her room. I'll be thinking of you all day today, even more
than I do every other day. I love you and miss you.

I didn't realize it until recently, but I had become accustomed to thinking that the best time of my life was the present. I think this belief started at the time I fell in love with Clare. In spite of the turmoil of ending my first marriage, each day, each month, each year brought something new to be happy about. Emily and Lucas were the final affirmations of the happiness I took as my due. I felt good about my age, even in the face of declining eyesight, hearing, and endurance. I became unafraid of getting older because of the promise that I would watch the two of them grow and become ever more remarkable people. Now half of that joy is gone, replaced by a sense of futility and impotence in the face of indifferent fate. I think back a year and can hardly believe that I accepted my sense of security as normal.

We begin to think now of our annual trip to the Bahamas in November. Since last we were there the small island we visit was devastated by Hurricane Andrew—and we have been struck by the more powerful storm of Lucas's illness and death.

SEPTEMBER 27, 1992

Clare and I put together a letter/proposal to send to various Baltimore family foundations in an effort to raise money for Lucas's memorial suite at the Tremont

Plaza. I think we'll need about $150,000 to fund the project in perpetuity. I hope we can raise it; it would be a wonderful way to preserve his memory. We can put some of his toys there and redecorate it for families from out of town whose children are at Hopkins.

SEPTEMBER 28, 1992

Today at work I saw a young woman who had been hospitalized in New York for two months. She has a panic disorder, and, in taking the history, I found she had graduated from Swarthmore with Andrew's class. I didn't know how to raise this issue until I finally asked her if she knew me "in another context." She replied, "Yes, I knew Andrew and what happened to him." I asked her if she thought this would interfere with our working together and was, in spite of myself, relieved to hear her say, "Yes, I think it might." I was able then, in good conscience, to refer her elsewhere. Small, painful world.

Emily is worried about Clare and me these days. She's having dreams about Lucas and fears for our health and safety. A natural apprehension, I suppose, but it's distressing to see the slow healing in her young life.

Clare bought me a bicycle. My first reaction was a reluctance to give up the old one and whatever connection to Lucas it represents. I took a long ride today and stopped by his grave to show him my new bike.

OCTOBER 7, 1992

I labor to write a paragraph or two each day about Lucas's life, trying to fix all my memories of him.

Emily said to Clare on Saturday, "Sometimes I can't believe he was really here." I know what she means. I look at his picture now and it is beyond my comprehension that he no longer lives on this earth except in our hearts. Clare took some rolls of film to be developed, and, unexpectedly, one of them contained some random pictures of the inside of the car that Lucas had apparently taken. It felt to us like a message about his continuing presence in which we so much want to believe. Also on the roll were a couple of wonderful pictures of Lucas and Emily together in the hospital.

OCTOBER 10, 1992

Today I received a call from David Talbot, editor of *Image,* the Sunday magazine at the *San Francisco Examiner.* They plan on running nearly the entire journal excerpt that I sent them—in two installments. I have mixed feelings about publishing this story. It feels like cutting open a vein in front of strangers.

I have thought a great deal about the role writing has played in getting through this. Knowing that there will be words in print about who he was and what he meant to us reassures me that a slender bond joins us still. If a few hearts can resonate to mine, perhaps we can share an understanding of what it means to love, to grieve, to be human.

OCTOBER 22, 1992

I've seen the galley proofs of the *Image* piece. They did an excellent job of editing and both halves of the story seem important: the purgatory of the hospital and the first four months of grieving. However others may react, I have fixed the experience in words.

OCTOBER 27, 1992

I hit a real low point last night and was critical of Clare for sleeping a lot and focusing only on work and Emily. Unforgivably, I also said I was angry with her "all the time." A little thought brought me closer to the truth: it's me that I'm really angry at. Just as I anticipated, the hardest part of this process is forgiving myself for my failure to save Lucas. I have no idea how to get past this, but taking it out on Clare, who loves me in spite of everything, is obviously not the way to do it. We reconciled with tears this morning and I took the day off. We needed time together to talk about our different ways of grieving. I find release in physical activity and an obsessive preoccupation with the fund-raising; Clare gains solace from her involvement with Emily's school and the peer counselors with whom she works at Johns Hopkins University who provide an additional focus for her maternal feelings. She is also more vulnerable to physical symptoms: headache, fatigue. I need to be more tolerant of these differences between us. We have lost our son; we must not lose each other.

OCTOBER 29, 1992

It is in the nature of grief that we cling to it even as it lacerates our hearts. It is the last connection to our loved one and, even in the face of the awful pain of remembering, we are loathe to let it go. Deeper than the silence of death is the fear of forgetting.

NOVEMBER 1, 1992

Halloween has come and gone. It was painful to remember Lucas last year in his knight's costume. Emily
slept over at Kathryn's, and Clare and I turned out the
lights and went to bed early.

NOVEMBER 5, 1992

The package containing the first issue of *Image* magazine came today with Lucas's smiling face on the
cover. I was crying when I finally reached Clare at
work. What will people think of my agony spread over
those pages? How can other families of sick children
take heart from what must seem a hopeless story?

I continue to solicit foundations for grants to his
memorial fund, twenty-two so far. I must give meaning to this loss or it will yet overwhelm me.

NOVEMBER 7, 1992

From Gary Kamiya, a senior editor at *Image* and the
person who did most of the editing on my journal, I
received an encouraging letter ("You have helped recall us to the humanity of the world"). He closed by
saying: "You and Clare and the rest of your family have
my deepest sympathy. I pray that, without ever forgetting your son, you find happiness and meaning in your
life again. I know you will. An angel will help you."

And so one person has responded to what I was trying to say in this story. Perhaps others will also and
Lucas's spirit will live on in some way in their hearts as
it does in mine.

All I really did was describe my pain. Lucas is
no more alive and my grief is hardly diminished by

whatever I might write. It is true, though, that my love for him was the purest act of my life. What is amazing is that I was capable of such emotion at all. It seems a modest act of hope that I have told others.

NOVEMBER 11, 1992

A man called me from San Francisco today. He had a son die from leukemia about ten years ago. He wrote a song about it and promised to send me a tape.

We go to the Bahamas next week—the one-year anniversary of our last innocent moments.

NOVEMBER 15, 1992

I went to church alone today, cried through most of it. There must be a bottom to this wellspring of tears. God knows when I'll reach it. Yesterday we went to the monument works that is preparing his headstone and gave our approval to the angel they have carved.

NOVEMBER 17, 1992

The *Examiner* forwarded some of the mail they received in response to the article and I have started to answer it. I was surprised at both the volume and the depth of feeling that the story seems to have evoked:

> I have never lost a child and Gordon Livingston has never lost a spouse, but his diary could easily have been mine. I cried for him, for his wife and daughter, and for me. May we all find peace!

There is incredible solace in knowing the pain of our loss is shared.

If it is true that we will all live on in the memories and deeds of those we leave behind, then Lucas lives through me now too and I thank his father for sharing his brief and brilliant son with me.

Dear Livingston Family, you are not alone.

I was greatly comforted by these responses. One parent of a child being treated for leukemia said that he was distributing copies of the article to the hospital staff. Another said that his first reaction was to hug his healthy young son. Perhaps, in the story of our loss and grief, there *is* embedded some universal message worth sharing. I hope so, else why bother?

One person who wrote found my journal irredeemably sad. But there are already books full of miraculous recoveries, many written by survivors, to give hope to families struggling with life-threatening illness. I wish I had such a story; it was the one I planned to write. Lacking that, I did what I could to pay tribute to my brave and beautiful son and to pass on to others some of the lessons about love that he taught me.

NOVEMBER 19, 1992

Today Clare and I went by the cemetery to see Lucas's newly erected monument: NEVER A CHILD MORE LOVED.

NOVEMBER 21, 1992

Now we are in the Bahamas. Kathryn is with us. Lucas is not. The people here have been kind, but I

feel only his absence—at supper and in our bed. In
retrospect, his tiredness here last year was the first
sign of the disaster that awaited. We are six months
past his death. Will this ache never diminish?

NOVEMBER 22, 1992

Today was typically bright and clear. We walked
into town, looking at the hurricane damage on the
way: roofs off, trees decapitated, walls down. We listened for a while outside the service at the Church of
God with its exuberant singing and dancing. I looked
at the tree, still standing, where Andrew took the photograph of the four of us, Lucas in my arms, that was
used in the magazine article. Then we walked back
along the beach with the east wind blowing and the big
waves rolling in from Africa. There are so many memories of him here from his six trips, starting when he
was two months old and lay in his infant seat on our
table at supper. I'm glad Emily has Kathryn to keep
her company. Tonight it looks like there will be a true
Bahamas sunset. I hope he's here watching over us.
Where else could he be?

NOVEMBER 23, 1992

From *Young Men and Fire* by Norman McClean:

If there is a story in Mann Gulch, it will take something of a storyteller at this date to find it, and it is not
easy to imagine what impulses would lead him to
search for it. He probably should be an old storyteller,
at least old enough to know that the problem of identity is always a problem, not just a problem of youth,
and even old enough to know that the nearest anyone

can come to finding himself at any given age is to find
a story that somehow tells him about himself.

Perhaps this is what Lucas's story has done for me.

We went scuba diving today, the four of us, to the
infamous "Devil's Backbone" upon which so many
ships have foundered. It was Emily and Kathryn's first
real dive and they were thrilled with the forty minutes
at twenty-five feet, circling among the coral. We saw
lots of yellowtails and one barracuda. Clare, having no
one to stay ashore with this year, went with us, her
first dive in a long time.

There is a special quiet to the evenings here, after
the sun has set but before true darkness is upon us. The
palm fronds sway in silhouette against the calm water
of the harbor. It is a time for reflection and memory. As
the last pinpoint of the sun disappeared over Eleuthera
this evening, I thought about distances and wondered
how far Lucas's spirit is from me. Is he hovering close
in the gentle Bahamian breeze or is he somewhere far
in the west with the sun? I hope he looks over my
shoulder and reads these words of love and longing.

McClean writes:

> Perhaps this is a reminder to keep open the possibility
> that there is no real ending . . . to the story. If so, then
> let it be so—there's a lot of tragedy in the universe
> that has missing parts and comes to no conclusion, in-
> cluding probably the tragedy that awaits you and me.

I have finished now this book about death in a wild-
fire of thirteen young smoke jumpers. McClean was an
old man when he wrote it, and moved to think of his
wife's death from cancer. I think of my children and my

struggle to make sense of existence. I imagine creating a new life and wonder if it is fair to do so when I feel so old. And yet, what is there in the universe to give it meaning except love and all its natural outcomes?

I looked back at my journal for a year ago and found only one entry from the Bahamas—about how much we felt Andrew's presence here. Even in the shadow of his death, how little I then knew of grief.

It would be an enormous comfort to me to believe that Clare's mother and Andrew and Lucas are together. It requires, no doubt, a simpleminded comprehension of the hereafter to imagine such a thing, but I wish for it nonetheless, especially now when we are in this place that meant so much to all of them. It seems to be at this time of day, near sunset, that I think with greatest puzzlement and sadness about my lost sons being somewhere without me. I have nearly given up on any clear reassurance from God about this.

NOVEMBER 26, 1992

Thanksgiving. I went on a dive with Emily and Kathryn this morning. We dove to eighty feet in coral canyons and encountered exotic fish. The girls appear to be having a wonderful time. Memories of Lucas occupy my mind. I don't want to talk to Clare about it; she seems at ease though she wears always a little golden angel on her blouse. I remember him waiting at the end of the dock when I returned from a dive. He waved as he saw me and jumped into my arms as we landed. He was here at this time every year of his life. It is amazing what we take for granted.

Tomorrow we go home. I think we leave behind a little of our grief in each of these places. We can never bury it all under new memories, nor do we want to. If only I can savor the six and a half years that he was with me and not focus on the many (or few) I must live without him.

Why is it that God makes it so difficult to believe in Him? If Lucas were here with us, if the transplant had worked, it would be so easy to comprehend a just Lord and his miracles. It is when I face the despair of my loss and the recurrent memories of my son's long death that, like Job, I am tempted to "curse God and die." But in saying that, I acknowledge His existence. Maybe this is the lesson of my unrequited hope: God does not show Himself by answering our prayers. Instead He challenges us to believe and to struggle on in the face of anger and grief. Perhaps that is the ultimate act of faith—to lose even those closest to us without losing our ability to love, still and again.

Even so, I continue to pray. At the waterfront tonight, I asked God to show me a shooting star if Lucas was okay. After about ninety seconds, He did.

NOVEMBER 29, 1992

We are home now after the long flight up the coast. The girls had a wonderful time, and the rebuilding of the island after the hurricane may have some parallels in our lives. The Christmas advertising blitz is on and will be hard to ignore or endure. A retreat to the mountains for the holidays seems to me the best strategy.

DECEMBER 5, 1992

Emily and Clare are in New York City for the Matisse exhibit. The silence of the house is a shroud cloaking my aloneness. What is left for me now? Lucas is gone. There is nothing to bind me to him except my memories. When I die, perhaps before, they too will be gone. The futility of my life weighs heavily upon me. Who will remember what I tried to do and be? What is there to tell? He wished to be a hero but, with all the love that was in him, could not save his first- and last-born sons.

As an antidote to despair I continue to send out fund-raising letters to corporations—so far with no results. I've gotten through *M* in a national directory (Mattel Toys). Getting money for the memorial fund has proven difficult. It seems important to persist, but $150,000 is a lot to raise.

I'm still receiving mail from California expressing support and sympathy and containing many stories of loss and grief.

DECEMBER 7, 1992

Today I had to go in to Hopkins for the first time since Lucas's death. One of my patients had surgery there and needed me. As I entered the hospital, I could not keep myself from looking up at that window on 3 South where our hopes burned to ashes.

The Chief of Pediatrics at Hopkins has written to ask if I will speak at the annual "Tribute Service" for families whose children have died during the past year. I don't know if I can bring anything useful to a room so full of grief, but maybe I should try. As a condition for doing so, I asked for an hour to speak with the pediatric caregivers. I *do* have some things I want to tell them.

DECEMBER 12, 1992

I feel so tired these days. The Christmas season, with its unremitting reminders of all that is joyful and childlike, weighs upon us. We are also approaching the anniversary of Lucas's death sentence. Can I ever enjoy this time of year again or will I grow embittered at the happiness all around me? I continue to distract myself with fund-raising. Things must get better next year; they could hardly be worse.

DECEMBER 19, 1992

We are past the one-year anniversary of Lucas's diagnosis. Christmas surrounds us and there is no escape. Clare has decorated his grave with pine boughs and red ribbon. We plan a few days' retreat to the mountains. All I want is to be alone with Clare and Emily in some place free of memories. Perhaps what I need to admit is that such a place does not exist.

DECEMBER 20, 1992

Today Clare and I went to church and it turned into the usual tearful experience. Later we put some battery-powered lights on the little Christmas tree in front of Lucas's headstone. We stopped by tonight to look at the pinpoints of brightness in the graveyard darkness. God, I will be glad to be done with this season.

We are on our way to the Virginia mountains. I
stopped by Lucas's grave to tell him we're leaving,
though I would like to believe that he's with us wherever we are. Clare found in his room a little figurine
that he had wrapped as a Christmas present last year,
then had forgotten to give her; on the card in his inimitable hand was "To Mom from Lucas." He had also
gotten a glass swan for his teacher, Michelle Kupiec,
but never gave it to her because he had to go back into
the hospital. Clare took it up to school and left it for
her with a note. The kids were preparing for their
Christmas concert.

DECEMBER 24, 1992

It is a strange Christmas Eve. Clare's sister Julie has
driven up from Atlanta and is staying with us. We
brought presents from home and want to make it a
happy time for Emily. Yet I have been thinking all day
of Lucas. I don't believe I'll ever recover the spirit of
this holiday without him. Clare came across his Christmas stocking at home while packing. How could he die
still believing in Santa Claus? In the evening light I can
see for miles past the mountains east to the coastal
plain. In a world so large and so full of tragedy it
seems self-indulgent to endlessly reflect on only one.
But I do, for it is my own.

It's Christmas Eve, Luke, and I miss you so. This, above
all such nights, faces me with your absence and my longing
to take you in my arms as I did so many times. I want to help
fill your stocking, to put away the milk and cookies left for
Santa, to look at the presents piled beneath the tree, and to

think of the joy of tomorrow. I can't do this tonight—or ever again.

As much as I will always miss you, it makes me happy that we were together for six-and-a-half years on the earth. I wish more than anything that our spirits will be joined again. Until then I hope you can feel me loving you, just as you could when you were here for me to hold. Sweet dreams.

DECEMBER 25, 1992

Christmas morning—the presents all opened. Emily was thrilled with her little battery-powered TV and the two angel statues that now rest on the mantel. The framed picture of herself and Lucas that she gave Clare brought some tears, but it was a generally happy morning in what feels like a faraway place. New Year's will be tough also, but somehow I feel the worst is over. It is a pleasure to focus all our energy and love on Emily.

DECEMBER 26, 1992

Sitting on this mountaintop, nursing still the open wound of Lucas's death, I think of the many stories that make up my life. I question which of these is worth telling —of any interest or meaning to others. It seems too late for many things, and I wonder at what point my mind or body will betray me and my storytelling days will end. It is a comfort, though, to have been able to speak through this journal of my love for my son. Perhaps, in the end, that *is* my story: the tale of a man, separate from others, whose futile, at times comical, efforts to define himself came down at last to the simple pleasure of loving his children.

I neglect, of course, in this construction, to mention the event that put an end, finally, to my confusion about my place in the world—falling in love with Clare. The intensity of passion and reassurance released in the act of loving and being loved by her made all else possible, including the realization of who I was and had always been. Even in the awful pain of Lucas's death, there has not been a moment of regret about the relationship that brought him to us. Giving myself to her was the defining moment of my life. In Lincoln's words, it remains "the certificate of my moral character."

JANUARY 1, 1993

We have come home to the memory of midnight, last January first at Hopkins, squeezed into that little room with the IV poles, holding Lucas on my lap, watching the fireworks over the Inner Harbor. Oh, to go back to that time—when all seemed possible and we were together.

Tonight Emily has three of her school friends here for a celebration and sleep-over. Clare and I went out to the grave and looked at his little lighted Christmas tree.

JANUARY 3, 1993

I believe that, on balance, I'm doing okay. I haven't given up on myself, those I love, or my search for God. I channel my energies into raising money for the memorial fund. I still have my sense of humor and my capacity for useful work. I try for courage but achieve only a sort of defiant resignation, a sense that the worst has befallen me and I am still here. If I cannot overcome fate, I can at least not be crushed by it.

Today I inventoried Lucas's room, a task that I had been putting off for weeks. We have kept his door closed but have not disturbed the contents. As I stood alone among his things I could feel his presence. There was a picture of him with Emily when he was two, a chart of "The World's Most Dangerous Sharks," a gingerbread house from his last Christmas, the "Star of the Week" poster, made by his kindergarten classmates containing their comments about him ("He is my friend," "He's the best person in the world," "We all like to play with Lucas."), his airplane lamp, a mirror that came from the house I grew up in. There are books too numerous to count, each one weighted with the memory of my reading it to him. I was flooded with longing as I felt the distance growing between us. He is not seven and that is no longer his room. I brought down to my office a small hourglass timer from some game or other; its twenty-second running time seems a fitting symbol of his brief stay on this earth—and a reminder of the small time left to me to love and to remember.

JANUARY 4, 1993

The Well of Grief

Those who will not slip beneath
  the still surface on the well of grief

turning downward into its black water
  to the place we cannot breathe

will never know the source from which we
    drink,
the secret water, cold and clear,

nor find in the darkness glimmering
  the small round coins
    thrown by those who wished for
    something else.

David Whyte

JANUARY 5, 1993

A man writes me from California. He has read my story and encloses a column about an eight-year-old boy in New York City about to be orphaned when his mother dies of AIDS. He thinks that my loss and the child's may be complementary and that we can save each other. I don't think so.

JANUARY 8, 1993

I find myself relinquishing the dream of another child. In the face of Clare's misgivings I have lost my nerve. So many things can go wrong that I can't bring myself to push farther and must sadly let go. Clare, sensibly I think, wants to pour her love into Emily and cannot risk having her heart broken again.

The published parts of this journal have become an issue between us since much of the reaction to it, from public and friends alike, has focused on my relationship with Lucas, my suffering, while not acknowledging Clare's closeness to him and the astonishing fortitude with which she has borne the pain of his loss. I feel I have let her down by not finding words to describe her central role in enduring what Frank Conroy called "this electric nightmare."

Because of the differences in the way people grieve, and because each partner is a reminder to the other of what they created and lost, it is clear to me why many marriages do not survive the death of a child. Ours, however, will.

Yesterday we received a tape that Clare had solicited from a psychic/medium in England by the name of Ronald Hearn. I listened with skepticism, but, in spite of myself, I took comfort from what he said.

First, he described Lucas with amazing accuracy considering that all Clare had sent him was a name and age. He spoke of his "gentle nature," his "fair hair," and his sense of humor. He identified by name our psychologist friend Barbara as someone who was important to him. At one point he said, "I see him now as an angel, little angel Lucas." He said he could feel that something would be written about Lucas and something would be done thereby to help others. He described him as happy, smiling and growing, and being looked after by other family members, including a child who had preceded him in death. He also twice said that "he sends his love to his daddy." He said that he could hear Lucas saying "ticktock"; I had just wound our grandfather's clock that morning, a process that fascinated Lucas and always reminded me of the times when I watched my own father do this.

Most important, these messages made Clare and Emily happy and left us all with a sense of hope that he is all right.

Clare took Lucas's Nintendo to his friend David, whose birthday is this week. It was such a wonderfully thoughtful and appropriate gift. When he opened it, David said, "Lucas showed me how to get from one world to another." He showed us all that.

The nights have a sameness about them. We read in bed, then Clare goes to sleep first because she has to rise at 6:30 to take Emily to school. I read some more and, feeling tired at last, turn out the light. I look up at the round fluorescent sticker on the ceiling that Lucas called his "moon" and a great feeling of emptiness washes over me. It is more than memory or grief; it is the certain knowledge that I am never going to recover fully from this, never stop missing him, never feel whole again in the way that I did with him lying beside me. Emily, of the three of us, is best at getting on with her life, investing herself in her friends, and reasonably expecting her parents to take care of her and themselves.

Sometimes at night I think about driving to the airport, getting into the airplane, and flying west at one thousand feet in the darkness, until I meet the mountains. It would happen near Frederick, where Clare and I were married, lending the end a certain symmetry. I could not, of course, inflict that upon my family, but the idea that I might thereby join Lucas fills me with anticipation. I have had patients who have lost children and told me of a wish to follow them. Now I understand.

Today marks one year since the bone marrow transplant decision. We took their advice, imagined that we could heal him in this magical way, and then watched helplessly while my marrow killed him. It has the feel of a Greek tragedy, with the protagonist brought low by his pride, punished by the gods for his desire to be like them.

FEBRUARY 20, 1993

Today's mail brought a $5,000 check from the Kimberly-Clark Foundation, courtesy of its president, George Everbach, my West Point classmate. We are nearing $60,000 in our fund-raising for the memorial.

FEBRUARY 27, 1993

I feel so fragile. At one moment I can work, laugh, make love to Clare. At another I am in tears. I cannot seem to reestablish a steady sense of direction for my life. The momentum of the years and the obligations of the moment propel me forward—but toward what? If death comes to us all in random order, then what does the struggle signify?

FEBRUARY 28, 1993

Another Sunday without going to church. Clare sleeps till noon and Emily has no enthusiasm for returning to that place where we said good-bye to Lucas. I continue to contribute money, visit Lucas's grave, and plow the church parking lot when it snows. But neither the liturgy, the congregation, nor a belief in God draws me back.

A friend sent me an essay from the *New York Times Book Review* entitled "When Bad Things Happen to Good Writers." In it, the author, Nancy Mairs, talks about the "literature of personal disaster" and concludes that it must be held to the same standard as any other genre, namely, the quality of the writing; the mere recounting of suffering is not enough. She also speaks of the purpose of such books: "Those writers who seek to console and hearten must make themselves and their anguish wholly transparent . . . in order to persuade the skeptical reader, through the very writing, that survival (at least till the last page) is possible." She goes on to quote a passage from Andre Dubus, a writer disabled when struck by a car:

> After the dead are buried, and the maimed have left the hospitals and started their new lives, after the physical pain of grief has become, with time, a permanent wound in the soul, a sorrow that will last as long as the body does, after the horrors become nightmares and sudden daylight memories, then comes the transcendent and common bond of human suffering, and with that comes forgiveness, and with forgiveness comes love.

Today I gave a talk in Baltimore to a group of adoptive parents. I took Emily. It was the first time she had heard me speak, and I loved having her there, seeing what I have done so many times. It was a warm and sunny Sunday. I have some life in front of me.

A patient of mine, whom I have known for many years, was operated on for lung cancer at the local hospital. I was visiting him last night when he was agitated and disoriented. Suddenly he looked at me and said, "I want to go to Johns Hopkins." Surprised, I asked him why. He said, "Because that's where you are." Where did that come from? How did he know that my heart was buried there in the PICU?

Clare's birthday. Lucas's gift to her last year was a glass angel, which was somehow broken in the hospital. When, after his death, she returned to the store to buy a replacement, they had gone out of business.

Today I spoke at Hopkins, first to the pediatric caregivers, later at a Tribute Service to parents whose children had died there over the past year. For the talk to the doctors and nurses, I projected a photograph of Lucas on the screen and said in part:

> This is a picture of our six-year-old son who died in the Pediatric Intensive Care Unit of this hospital on May 19th, 1992. I thank you for coming. I know it can't be easy to subject yourselves to the pain of a bereaved parent on top of all your other responsibilities.
>
> You all deal daily with sick children and their families, yet I daresay that there are few among you who have any clear idea of what that experience is like from the family's point of view. I know that I didn't. I

spent my internship at a hospital where, during part of it, I cared for dying children. Perhaps it was that experience that moved me away from pediatric surgery toward a specialty that carries with it the risk of sudden death, but one where I am generally spared the spectacle of watching the best hopes of a family slowly reduced to ashes by a relentless disease beyond the reach of all that medicine has to offer. Those of you who are parents can perhaps come close to imagining the enormity of such an event. *Our* experience suggests that a common caregiver reaction is to withdraw and defend oneself from the pain and defeat that such a loss represents. This is not hard to do when the demands on your time are so great. There are vital signs to be monitored, dressings to be changed, lab values to be analyzed, other patients demanding attention. The frightened bystanders that parents become are in some ways impediments to the real business of the hospital: medicines, procedures, chemotherapy protocols, teaching. I remember the only half-facetious quote from my medical school days that "if it weren't for the patients the hospital could run a lot more efficiently."

If I sound cynical, I don't mean to. During the five months following his diagnosis, Lucas was hospitalized six times, on the last occasion for sixty-one days for a bone marrow transplant. During those hospitalizations we encountered many caregivers. Nearly all of them gave much of themselves to us and to our son—some of them far beyond their clinical responsibilities. What I really intend, therefore, is not to criticize those who fell short of this ideal. What I wish is to give you a glimpse of the hospital experience from the perspective of the family of a sick and ultimately dying child—what helped us and what didn't—so that you can perhaps take a little of what I say back to those children and families who so desperately need your skills, compassion, and understanding.

Throughout his illness we believed that the more optimistic and determined Lucas and we were in the face of his disease, the better his quality of life and *possibly* his chances of survival. We attempted therefore to create a healing environment in which all who were in contact with him conveyed a hopeful spirit, defied bad news, and assumed that, whatever happened, whatever the statistics, he was going to be an "exceptional patient." As a psychiatrist I am aware of the phenomenon of denial, and to some extent the idea of creating such a healing attitude requires some denial that a bad outcome is possible. This conviction, of course, does not involve the withholding of treatment; it simply assumes that how he and our family confronted the disease could have a favorable effect on outcome.

While we did not encounter any outright disagreement with this approach to Lucas's illness, neither did we sense a lot in the way of understanding how critical such a belief was to the maintenance of our morale. The emphasis of staff, especially doctors, seemed to be on lab values, vital signs, chemotherapy doses—all the routines of modern technological care. In general, the staff patiently answered our numerous questions. What we began to realize, however, was that the practice of pediatric oncology, with its many bad outcomes, carries with it a mind-set in which there seems to be a fear of overoptimism. It was as if everyone feared promising too much, so that it would be a mistake to be hopeful when so many things could go wrong. I also understand that there is a defense mechanism operating here, that after a few deaths people learn how to reserve a part of themselves so they can continue to function. This self-protective tendency was generally not expressed as directly as by the PICU nurse who told Clare that "I couldn't work here if I thought of them as children." Usually, we just got the sense of withholding full involvement with the family, and care taken to underscore the possible serious outcomes of each new crisis. Sometimes I could not but wonder if some of the caregivers were depressed at some level by the psychological burden imposed by daily contact with sick and dying children.

I don't want to get carried away by this point, because, in general, we felt that Lucas received wonderful and, at times, loving care from those on whom we so depended. I am just asking you to examine your hearts to see if anything I have said about the importance of caregiver attitudes and the nontechnical aspects of your interactions with families sounds as though it might apply to you.

Here seems a proper time to pay tribute to the amazing nursing staff on 3 South with whom we spent the last two months of Lucas's life. Many of them formed an attachment to us and to him that left us with the feeling they were holding nothing back and saw in him the same specialness of which we were so aware. For making themselves vulnerable to our suffering, we are grateful beyond measure.

It was not until a pulmonary consultant diagnosed a lung infiltrate and suggested bronchoscopy and transfer to the PICU that we really felt the situation spiral out of control. Naturally, the culture results from the bronchoscopy were rendered unreadable by some problem in the lab. He was placed on a respirator and floated in and out of consciousness for the last nine days of his life. Now you may say that this reflected the inevitable downward course of his GVHD, but we feel to this day that his precipitate removal from his place of safety on 3 South to the PICU contributed to his inability to fight back any longer. The change for the family was also disorienting; the limitations on visiting hours and number of visitors horrified us. To their credit, the nursing staff of the PICU made exceptions and for this I thank them. And here is another lesson I would ask you to take away from our experience: If the rules don't make sense, break them. At 11:00 P.M. that first night in the PICU, we were asked to leave. When we protested that this was a child who had not been without one of us for a moment during his hospitalization, the nurse in charge, to our relief, said we could stay. We had to look around for chairs to sit in, but at least we were there.

Then ensued an episode that illustrates the frustration of parents who know their child and his reactions to medication in a way no one else does, and yet are not listened to. It was decided to put Lucas on an antibiotic that had caused him severe nausea before. When Clare told this to the PICU resident and recommended something to control this side effect, he brushed the suggestion off by saying, "He won't get nauseated; we're giving the antibiotic IV." Lucas spent the rest of that night vomiting, over and over. This incident has assumed tremendous importance for us, not just because the doctor didn't listen, but because on the last night we had to communicate with our son before he was intubated and forever silenced, he could only retch and beg for water.

Lucas began to bleed from both his upper and lower GI tracts. After five days of every conceivable medical intervention, we turned to our psychologist friend Barbara, who had worked with Lucas throughout his illness on visualization. She made a tape asking him to stop the bleeding; we played it to him and he did. His ammonia level began to rise. We placed our hands on his abdomen and asked him to lower it. In the middle of the night, a new result came back showing an unexplained drop of 100 points. The nurse's immediate interpretation was "lab error."

Take our story with you and use it as you will. Thank you for your attempts to save our son. We blame no one. Our only wish is that my recounting a part of our ordeal may contribute in some way to your ability to convey the gifts of understanding and hope to those who prayerfully place in your hands their precious children.

As you can see, it was difficult for me to come back here today. I am reminded of photographs of Hiroshima after the war. There were shadows on the walls of buildings left by people who had been vaporized by the atom bomb. This is how I feel about Hopkins. The searing emotional experience of Lucas's death has left indelible images of our having been here. I will return sometimes to look at them and remember who I once was, but can never be again. Likewise, those with eyes to see and hearts to care will perhaps find the shadows of Lucas and all who loved him permanently and together a part of this place.

I barely got through it. Others wept as well, so perhaps the anguish of speaking of these things was worth it. Somehow the Tribute Service with the bereaved parents was easier, made so by their understanding, refined in fires of loss and grief. I closed with this prayer: *May we all find peace in the shared hope that our children who brought us such joy with their short lives are now a host of angels, loving us still, feeling our love for them, awaiting our coming, and knowing that they are safely locked forever in our hearts.*

MARCH 20, 1993

I can talk about him now in a fairly even way. I don't miss him less; it just seems that a sort of resignation is setting in. Today is the one-year anniversary of the hospitalization at the start of the transplant process. In two more months we will have finished the first year of grieving.

MARCH 21, 1993

Today we flew to Vermont for a four-day ski vacation. It puts me in mind of our trip to Killington with Lucas two years ago. Emily had learned to ski when she was five, so we tried to interest him in trying. We got as far as getting him suited up and fitted with rental skis. I helped him onto the chairlift and we went to the top of the beginner's slope. Just as we got off the lift, a photographer waiting there took a wonderful picture of Lucas looking like a veteran skier. Moments later he fell down and refused to ski anymore, even when I held him between my legs. I took off his skis and Clare carried them while I skied down the hill holding him in my arms. I remember thinking that there would be plenty of chances for him to learn.

MARCH 22, 1993

I skied this morning with Emily; Clare joined us this afternoon and was tearful on the first lift ride because of the reminders of Lucas. Once she began skiing, however, she enjoyed it, even when she fell down—to Emily's amazement and delight at the unaccustomed sight of her beautiful, competent mother making a mistake. All in all, it was a wonderful day and I felt that a bit more healing had taken place; now we can do *this* together without being overwhelmed by his memory.

It snowed overnight—about five inches. We all skied this morning. I do, of course, have people to live for and work to do. I should be praying for the strength to do it rather than endlessly feeling bereaved. I think once we're past May—the first year— the process of looking back will change from "What were we doing last year at this time?"

The world here is covered in white. Tomorrow we fly back to the warmth of a Maryland spring, washed clean by the rains. The crocuses will be raising their heads over the grave of my son.

MARCH 27, 1993

There was a moment on the flight back from Vermont when we passed just west of Albany. The visibility was nearly unlimited, and I could see Troy across the river. I was finally able to pick out the green water tower a block from the house where I grew up. I could see my high school and the V.A. hospital where my father worked and later died. I thought how much had passed in my life since the days when that was my world.

APRIL 1, 1993

This is the worst period of one-year anniversaries: the transplant on March 28 and the subsequent long, losing fight. When I think of us imprisoned in that hospital last year, watching our hopes slowly wither, it fills me with a sense of futility. Yet I remember also how close Lucas and I were, how much we held and loved each other.

A friend of Clare's is visiting from Boston with her three-year-old son, who warmed to me quickly and takes the same delight in the simple tickling games that Lucas did. He is such a cute, bright little boy. He kept asking me to read to him, and the feel of him nestled beside me was almost too much to bear. He sleeps in Lucas's room tonight, plays with his stuffed animals, reads his books. Lucas would like that.

APRIL 11, 1993

Easter. From the time Lucas could walk we had an Easter egg hunt in the backyard for him and Emily— some eggs easily found for him, others more difficult for her. They searched the area until all the eggs were picked up, then asked us to hide them again. The last hunt took place in his hospital room at Hopkins after his bone marrow transplant when he could still get out of bed. It was April 19 and he had one month to live.

APRIL 12, 1993

Emily asked me to go up to the field near the middle school today to throw the lacrosse ball around. She's gotten remarkably good since last year and is co-captain of her team. Then, after supper we shot some baskets in the driveway. I realized again tonight how proud of her I am, of her intelligence, of her skill at sports, of her wondrous spirit. It is such a pleasure to be part of her blossoming and it keeps me rooted to the world.

APRIL 17, 1993

I dreamed about Lucas last night. We were again in the PICU, and again he died. This time, however, in

the way of dreams, we were somehow allowed to
undo the bone marrow transplant and he was saved.
When I awoke, he was not beside me.

The cherry tree is in bloom outside the window and
spring has truly arrived. Bees flit among the blossoms.
We missed this moment last year, confined to the hospital fighting for Lucas's life. Emily sits in my soft chair
in the living room doing her homework. I hardly use it
anymore; I have too many memories of Lucas crawling
into my lap there, asking me to read him a book.

APRIL 25, 1993

Emily seems to be doing wonderfully in every part
of her life, but I worry about delayed or hidden reactions to Lucas's death. He does not appear to be at the
forefront of her mind as he is in mine. I notice each
morning, though, the collection of angels on the shelf
in her room.

It was a beautiful day, temperature in the high sev-
enties. I biked out to his grave and sat there a long
time. The leaves are out on the tulip poplar, but it has
not yet blossomed as it will by May 19. I am thinking
of canceling work this Thursday and flying up to Con-
necticut on the second anniversary of Andrew's death.
With six children, it seemed like a constant string of
birthdays; now I have two other dates to remember.

MAY 1, 1993

Yesterday, Clare and I went to morning assembly at
Emily's school and stood in the back to wait for the
announcement of next year's middle school president.
We had been called by the Head of School to let us

know that Emily had easily won the election. Some eighth graders put on a skit that showed the current president traveling to the Virgin Islands, where she decides to stay. It ended then with the need for a new president, and, shouting Emily's name, they rushed to her with a banner, balloons, hugs. Amid the cheers, I felt myself for a change shedding tears of joy.

Now we are in May and that awful anniversary stares at me from the calendar. But we are together, loving Lucas, one another, and even, from time to time, life itself.

MAY 2, 1993

A writer in Columbia sent me an excerpt from Shakespeare's *Venus and Adonis:*

> If he be dead,——O no, it cannot be,
> Seeing his beauty, thou shouldst strike at it;——
> O yes, it may; thou hast no eyes to see,
> But hatefully at random dost thou hit.
> Thy mark is feeble age; but thy false dart
> Mistakes that aim, and cleaves an infant's
>   heart.
>
> Hadst thou but bid beware, then he had
>   spoke,
> And hearing him, thy power had lost his
>   power.
> The Destinies will curse thee for this stroke;
> They bid thee crop a weed, thou pluck'st a
>   flower:
> Love's golden arrow at him should have fled,
> And not Death's ebon dart, to strike him
>   dead.

Dost thou drink tears, that thou provokest
  such weeping?
What may a heavy groan advantage thee?
Why hast thou cast into eternal sleeping
Those eyes that taught all other eyes to see?
Now Nature cares not for thy mortal vigour,
Since her best work is ruin'd with thy rigour.

"Those eyes that taught all other eyes to see." Oh,
Luke!

a seed on the wind

The death of a child is a fire in the mind. The mind burns with alternatives that never come to pass, with fantasies of remarkable recuperations, with dreams of adult accomplishment. If we let this fire burn compassionately within us, the grief of the mind, the fantasies, the burning of the spirit, begin slowly to melt away and the child comes more into our heart. Our anguish can be used to open more fully, to enter as completely as we can into this final sharing. And then, as Rabindranath Tagore wrote in the final lines of his poem, *The End,* "Dear Auntie will come with presents and will ask, 'Where is our baby, Sister?' and Mother, you will tell her softly, 'He is in the pupils of my eyes. He is in my bones and in my soul.'"

Stephen Levine
Who Dies?

MAY 3, 1993

Gary Hart, in a recent magazine interview, said that when he is recognized on the street and asked if he is Gary Hart, he replies, "I used to be." I feel the same way. I used to be Lucas's father. Now I'm one of the walking wounded.

MAY 9, 1993

Mother's Day. The cycle of the seasons has brought us round to this most beautiful time. When I think of where we were last year, in the PICU watching Lucas slip away from us, I wonder what it means to heal. Emily wrote her mom a wonderful poem today and I brought her flowers. Together we gave her a set of angel earrings. I just realized that Lucas died between Mother's Day and Father's Day.

MAY 12, 1993

As I was running this evening, two little boys, six or seven years old, were riding their bikes on the pathway near the elementary school. One of them was having trouble staying up and I held his seat and ran with him until we reached his turnoff. "Now you can let go," he said. I did and he rode away from me, balancing on his own.

MAY 15, 1993

Clare is devoting time to beautifying Lucas's grave and is planning a memorial garden with a fountain in the backyard.

Emily and I traveled to Swarthmore Sunday for a tree-planting arranged by Andrew's roommate, Gary. *Franklinia alatamaha* was the young tree chosen, reputed to have wine-red leaves in the fall. The site is on the south lawn of the observatory near a well-traveled walkway. For the inscription on the plaque I chose a quote from Thomas Mann.

In Memory of
Andrew Lowry Livingston
1968–1991

—

Hold every moment sacred.

At work today, a patient, seeing the pictures on my desk, asks how many children I have. "Six," I quickly reply.

MAY 18, 1993

Clare has decorated Lucas's grave site with azalea bushes, impatiens, and statues of angels at rest. I pray that my sons are together in peace and happiness, and can feel my love everlasting. Lucas died a year ago tomorrow; Clare and I are both taking the day off—to do what I'm not sure. Perhaps just to remember.

MAY 19, 1993

How does one mark such an anniversary? We have lived through each season now without our son. It was a dismal, rainy morning as I drove Emily to school.

She did not mark the day and I was grateful to be able to talk with her of other things: whether her lacrosse practice would be canceled, what tests she had to prepare for. I needed the reminder of all that I still have on this day when my mind is on what I have lost.

Clare and I went out to lunch and recalled some times with Lucas, most of them funny, and shared a hope that the next year will be easier. We spoke of summer plans: Clare and Emily will go to England next month to visit Ronald Hearn, the psychic who amazed us with his tape. Even though I would like to meet him, I decided not to go. I told Clare that I was too immersed in the fund-raising. I could not speak my real, irrational fear: that England is just too far away from Lucas. We decided that we could not yet face a vacation at Squam Lake in New Hampshire, that lovely place so full of happy memories.

Later in the afternoon we sat silently together on the bench by his grave. Our thoughts were our own; these were mine: The blossom-weighted tulip branch hangs low over this place as it did one year ago. The spring rain mingles with my tears to water the new grass. The pain is different now, just as he would be, just as I am. Where is the little boy for whom I weep? On the stone is an angel. In my heart his smiling face is engraved forever. The rain falls. The tree blooms. I wait.

MAY 24, 1993

I am building a cardboard boat. Each of the last three years the city has sponsored a "regatta" for human-powered boats made of corrugated cardboard. The challenge, of course, is to waterproof the cardboard enough to keep from sinking while paddling around a two-hundred-yard course. In a very simple craft, Emily and I made the semifinals two years ago. Last year we were otherwise occupied. This time I have designed a thirteen-foot, two-person kayak that looks to me as though it will move at a respectable speed. It's a wacky idea to be sure, but therein lies its charm; so I measure, cut, fold, and paint cardboard in the garage. Clearing a space big enough to do so, I uncovered many of Lucas's toys and stuffed animals.

MAY 29, 1993

We just learned that the father of Amy, the little girl who died in the PICU one week after Lucas, was struck by a moving train three days ago on the first anniversary of her death. He sustained a broken arm and a head injury. I guess I'm not the only one finding it difficult to go on.

MAY 31, 1993

It is hard to conceive of heaven because, while Lucas was alive, I felt the closest to that state that I can imagine. Much of the pleasure that I remember was imagining our relationship growing and changing. Even if our souls meet again, I cannot possibly have that experience. And how will I be marked by the rest of my life? Does the spirit age with the body? These unanswerable questions weigh heavily as I struggle to understand all that has happened.

Today there was a tree-planting ceremony at
Stevens Forest Elementary. Michelle Kupiec, Lucas's
teacher, brought out some of the first-graders who
had been his classmates. The principal recalled when
a musical group came to the school to perform for the
kids. They asked if anyone knew "Amazing Grace."
Lucas, who had heard it at Andrew's funeral, raised
his hand and joined the group on stage until he became too shy and sat down. The tree is a "weeping
cherry"—Lucas had been in a section of the school
called Cherry Team—and it was planted just outside the
fence near the kindergarten. Michelle read a poem she
had written:

> Lucas Livingston
> Here in the calm of this lush day of spring,
> our hearts commune in remembering
> Dear Lucas, a gentle and loving boy,
> whose time with us here brought special joy.
> He loved reading to Pooh Bear and watching
>   Loony Tunes,
> and coming to school in the afternoons,
> riding on the back of his daddy's moped,
> a miniature helmet perched on his blond head.
> Lucas delighted in life's simple pleasures;
> he generously shared his greatest treasures.
> The swan night-light he wrapped for me,
> and hid under his bed so no one would see.
> But I saw the beauty of a giving spirit,
> I thank God every day I had the chance to be
>   near it.
> God gave us Lucas, so precious and mild,
> our angel on earth, this soft-spoken child.

No matter what happened, Lucas looked for
   the best;
he showed us all that we were blessed.
I was touched by his life for a little while.
I held him and loved him and was healed by
   his smile.
To honor Lucas's memory,
we come together to plant a tree.
Outside my window,
it will stretch toward the sky.
Each time I look out,
I'll feel him nearby.

I read the Stevenson poem "In Memoriam," Clare
gave everyone a bookmark with Lucas's picture, and
each of us shoveled a spadeful of dirt into the hole.
Leaning against the tree were left the words that I
chose to go on the plaque to be placed there:

In Memoriam

LUCAS SCOTT LIVINGSTON

1985–1992

—

Undiminished gladness,
Undeparted dream.

Two sons, two trees.

JUNE 12, 1993

Today Emily and I capsized rounding the second
buoy in the cardboard-boat regatta, the result of faulty
design work on the kayak that I will attempt to correct
next year. The rescue boat rushed over and threw me

a flotation ring, hardly necessary in view of the fact that 1. I was already wearing a life jacket, and 2. I was standing on the bottom. Emily took our pratfall with her usual good spirits ("Oh, Dad, it was too hot to paddle anyway.")

At the lakefront is an area paved several years ago with hundreds of named bricks. I went over and looked at the one that says EMILY AND LUCAS LIVINGSTON.

JUNE 17, 1993

Today, Andrew's birthday, I flew to New Haven. Nina and Michael met me at the airport and dropped me off at the cemetery, where I spent a half-hour alone near the body of my first son. There is new grass on his grave and I brought some fresh flowers. Seeing his name and the dates of his life carved on the stone lent a finality to his death in the same way that I remember when I saw the names of young men I had known on my first trip to the Vietnam Memorial. Andrew was with me that day as I cried unexpected tears. Today I wept for him—and for myself. His death is a door forever slammed in our faces.

His mother joined me there. She is having trouble forgiving herself as are we all. I try to get her to see his bipolar illness as a sort of malignancy that destroyed him.

I visited the tree where he died and left a flower there. It is an oak at the top of a wooded hill with a limb suited to his purpose. When did he see this, pick it out as his hanging tree, imagine himself climbing to its first large fork, then leaning out to tie the bowline around the limb before launching himself into eternity? What was he thinking? Did he leap from this world with a final surge of control, embracing oblivion? Did his soul make a sound as it ascended, finally free, from the body that held all we loved of him?

I tried to evoke his presence today, but, though I spoke to his grave and to his dying place, I could not feel him there. His mother told me of a firefly coming toward her one evening, unblinking, turning away like an airplane. Andrew had gotten his pilot's license when he was eighteen and she said he had later told her that he regretted that he could no longer fly. Now perhaps, a weightless spirit, he can.

JUNE 18, 1993

Dear Andrew,

You shouldn't have done this. Your life, hard as it had become, was precious to a lot of people. None of our lives are completely our own to dispose of as we wish. We all have connections that are claims on our humanity and demand weight in our every decision—especially the choice to live or die.

I miss you. As I stood by the tree yesterday I thought of your last moments, forever unknowable. Did you hesitate, contemplating the awful pain your death would bring to those who loved you? There has to be some meaning to this loss beyond the random inheritance of a bipolar gene. You were so much more than that illness. You were loved, Andrew, and that this was not enough to sustain you, that perhaps you couldn't even feel it clearly, is sad beyond any consolation.

Beside your bed was a photograph of me at your age that I gave your mother many years ago. I was wearing my West Point dress uniform. On the back, in my handwriting, was a

single Latin word: spero—*I hope. I wonder now what it was
I was hoping for. Perhaps that I would never have to face a
moment like this. Was my picture one of the last things you
looked at before driving to the woods?*

*Over the last few days the lyrics of an old Tom Paxton song
have been playing in my head:*

> *Are you going away with no word of farewell?*
> *Will there be not a trace left behind?*
> *I could've loved you better,*
> *Didn't mean to be unkind.*
> *You know that was the last thing on my mind.*

JUNE 20, 1993

Father's Day again. On the wall of our room is a
homemade card from Father's Day two years ago: a
heart with an angel sticker affixed and the words "I
love you Dad. Love, Lucas."

JUNE 25, 1993

> I thought I heard my son laugh tonight.
> My heart stopped a moment
> As I listened again for that sound.
> But it was not he,
> Only a friend of his sister's
> Staying the night.
> It could not have been Lucas,
> Not my son,
> In his grave a year now,
> Lost to modern medicine
> And my bone marrow.
> They come in moments like this,
> Memories unbidden,
> Of what it was like

To hear him laugh,
Body and spirit.
Before the cell deep within him
Mutated
And sent us spinning into the world
Of hospitals, chemotherapy, transplants,
And Death.
Someday, I pray
To hear that laugh again.
And this time
Have it be him
Forever.

JUNE 28, 1993

Today at work I received a phone message from Jenny, a young single mother of a six-year-old boy, Alec, who has been in the Hopkins PICU for three weeks. He is sixty days post–bone marrow transplant and has a fungal infection that has compromised his breathing. The doctors have told her that he is going to die. Jenny read an article I had written about Lucas for *Baltimore* magazine and "needed to talk to someone who had been through this." She feels that Alec is a lot like Lucas in his sweetness and concern for others. At one point in his three-year struggle with T-cell lymphoma, he took her face in his hands and said, "Don't worry, Mom, wherever you are, I'll always be there."

"Do you ever get over this?" she asked tearfully. I tried to console her but realized that Clare could do it better and I got them in contact. When next I spoke with Clare she had decided, in an act of incredible bravery, to go to the PICU to be with Jenny. Tonight she described the scene: the little boy unconscious, his mom holding onto whatever hope she could still muster, the awful feel of that place of despair. How much random sadness this world contains. Clare rented a hotel room for Jenny's parents, who live about five hours away.

JUNE 30, 1993

It's just past midnight and I celebrated the advent of my fifty-fifth birthday by taking a bucket of water up to the weeping cherry in front of the kindergarten at Lucas's school. It's a small tree, and we haven't had rain in ten days, so each night I take water. The laminated bookmark with Lucas's picture and the Fulghum poem ("And I believe that love is stronger than death") is attached to the trunk.

Clare received a call from Alec's grandmother at Hopkins this evening to say that he had died. Another triumph of modern medicine. Now his poor mother is at last freed, as we were, from the imprisonment of the PICU. God help us all.

While going through a book last night, Clare came across an "angel gift"—a multicolored card with balloons and streamers and two dogs, one large, one small, wearing party hats:

TO MY DADDY ON HIS BIRTHDAY,

> *Inside:* It's fun to have a daddy
> As wonderful as you—
> You're extra special,
> extra nice,
> And I sure love you, too!
> HAPPY BIRTHDAY
> X O X O
> L U ⊃ A S

His name was written with a backward C, so he must have given it to me when he was five. Clare did her best to celebrate the day with me: movie, dinner, chocolate-chip cookie. Emily called from France where she is on a bike trip organized by her school. Four more days and she'll be home and I can feel like a father again.

At our request, Claire Femiano, Lucas's nursery school teacher, dictated her memories of him. Some excerpts from her tape:

> Lucas had a kind heart. Sometimes I'd get him to do a cooking project by telling him that, even though *he* didn't want to eat it, I wished he would just make it for me so that I wouldn't be hungry for a snack. Most times, this would work.
>
> Emily was very special to him. I remember that a couple of times when we would give out treats for the kids, he'd ask if he could have an extra one for Emily. You think that probably most kids do that; but truth be told, they don't. One time when we made an egg book that took a lot of work, he proudly announced that he was going to give it to Emily.
>
> Humor played an interesting part in Lucas's life. I remember him telling me about his favorite TV show, "America's Funniest Home Videos." I'll never forget how he could remember, word-for-word, action-for-action, what happened in that show. He laughed uproariously as he described the tapes and seemed so glad to share them with me.
>
> One time the kids were asked to bring in something that their parents used on their job. Lucas came in with a hammer. I said, "Lucas, does Dad use this on his job?" He explained what the hammer was used for

and said, "Yep, yeah, my Dad uses this on his job." My assistant and I had a good laugh over that, trying to relate psychiatry to a hammer. It was so cute.

In January of Lucas's second year in school, my husband had a serious accident and for a time it was difficult for me to work. Lucas developed a little ritual to help start the day: he would come in, look around the room and search me out, run up to me, and give me the biggest, brightest smile and say "Hi, Claire." I would respond, "Hi, Lucas," and I feel so lucky that I have such a clear picture in my mind of that smile. This went on for many weeks and I didn't realize at the time how much that ritual helped me make it through the day. Looking back, could he have somehow sensed that I was sad and needed something to perk me up? I don't know. I do know that as the weeks went on and my husband healed, the ritual stopped. I regret somehow never thanking Lucas for cheering me up when I needed it, but I doubt he would have understood what I was thanking him for. I think he was simply an angel, heaven-sent.

JULY 3, 1993

And now, it seems, I will collect these memories into a book in the inevitably vain attempt to capture the spirit and image of my son. Even though I fall short, I think I must try, because he was the vessel into which I poured the dream of what I wanted my life to be. He was loving, kind, strong, and full of laughter. All these qualities deserve celebration and remembrance. As long as those who loved him are alive, his spirit cannot die, but I want more for him—and me. I wish for a kind of immortality that will dignify both our lives, his so short and mine longer than I deserve. What he and I were to each other speaks of all the meaning that life can contain. It is a tale that deserves telling, not because it is new or unique, but because it is old and commonplace and embodies that which gives value to our time on earth. Perhaps I can find some words to render this truth visible to some who would otherwise not see it—so that they may in their lives cleave to those they love, as did Lucas and I, and be ennobled thereby.

JULY 4, 1993

I am where I was last year at this time, at my desk listening to the fireworks at the lake. Am I any further along in trying to find some meaning in what has befallen us? I think so. I have written, I have spoken, I have wept. And people, some of them, have listened. Mostly I have endured, loved those who need me, and not surrendered to the heavy hand of fate.

Today Emily returned from her seventeen-day bicycle trip in France. She looks beautiful and fit and happy after her 450-mile odyssey. She exudes an expanded view of herself and what she can do.

The following letter from a friend was published in our local newspaper:

A SISTER'S LOVE WAS A COMFORT TO LUCAS

The article about the life and death of six-year-old Lucas Livingston was extremely moving.

There is another aspect of the story, however, that should be mentioned. It is the quality of the relationship between Lucas and his sister Emily.

Two weeks before Lucas died, I picked Emily up from school and drove her to Hopkins to see her brother. She visited him for several hours each day.

As the elevator arrived on the floor where Lucas was, Emily seemed to disconnect from me and her surroundings. With a quickened step she moved down the long corridor to his room. Upon seeing Lucas, she tenderly embraced his terribly ill body. She whispered that she wanted to tune in his special cartoons on the hospital room TV.

Emily then told him what had happened at school and gently asked how his day had been. Even in his critically ill state, Lucas turned to her. There was an indescribable rapport that only these two loving children could understand.

JULY 8, 1993

Tonight, since we are in the midst of a heat wave with little rain for two weeks, I went out to Lucas's grave to water the flowers. There was a new little headstone near his:

ZACHARY GOODWIN

Our Little Angel

Feb. 23, 1993

There were two small pebbles on Lucas's monument that had not been there before. I am so glad that people visit and that we have made the place beautiful. One visitor described it as "a shrine."

JULY 14, 1993

Emily and Clare called tonight from London. They seem to be having a wonderful time. Emily said that today they had been to see Ronald Hearn, the psychic, and that it was reassuring. I suppose I should be there, but I feel somehow that I am needed here. For what reason though? Lucas cannot be here any more than with them in England. Perhaps, in the way of spirits, he can be everywhere.

Alone, I live an economical life. I have always, at bottom, been a solitary person and there is really no one or nothing that I wish to see except for Clare, Emily—and Lucas. What is it that has kept me separate from the rest of humankind? My one satisfaction is that those I have loved, I have loved well. Perhaps the best epitaph to which I can aspire will be: He never figured it out, but he never ceased to try.

JULY 21, 1993

> Life has meaning only in the struggle,
> Triumph or defeat is in the hands of God.
> So let us celebrate the struggle!
>
> Swahili warrior song

JULY 24, 1993

Emily has decided not to go away to camp for a week in August. She also announced her intention to go to college at Hopkins. I guess, after all the traveling, she's feeling a bit of separation anxiety. It's so good to have her around. We tossed the lacrosse ball for a while today, then watered the flowers on Lucas's grave. I think I'm starting to feel lucky again.

JULY 30, 1993

Today I went in to Baltimore to tape a television interview show—yet another effort to tell Lucas's story and make an appeal for funds for the memorial.

I went out with Emily tonight to split some oak firewood from a tree that blew down. It somehow seemed important to me that she have a memory of her dad swinging a nine-pound sledge. It's one of the many skills I hoped to teach Lucas—about chain saws and firewood and splitting with a wedge. Such things are naturally not of much interest to Emily, but now she has a picture that I hope will come to her sometime in the future as she sits around a hardwood fire.

AUGUST 7, 1993

The interview that I taped last week was on TV tonight. I watched myself looking stricken and old and speaking of hope, though truthfully I feel little—other than the hope that people will send money for the memorial. Who am I to speak of meaning, the father of two dead sons? The best I can do is stare this calamity in the face and find some reason to live.

AUGUST 15, 1993

Today I came to a realization that seems important to me: the body and the spirit age at different rates. I should have known this, for I have seen very old spirits in very young bodies and vice versa. In my own case the distinction is important because of my sense that I have grown old rapidly since Lucas's death. This, I now realize, has been an aging of the spirit brought on by grief and withered hopes. My body does not feel young anymore, but neither is it old. I can still run, split wood, throw a lacrosse ball, ride my bike. If, however, I am to realign body and spirit it will take some doing. If I can find some faith and purpose, perhaps in just telling this story, then maybe I can slow the process of spiritual aging. This seems to me something worth striving for.

We are in Wyoming again; tonight we went to the rodeo. At one point they let all children under twelve go into the arena and chase three calves, trying to capture a ribbon attached to the tail of each. There were dozens of blond-headed boys, scampering about, oblivious to everything except the fun of pursuing those calves.

At one point my niece reached over to take something from her mother. I found myself, to her surprise, reaching up to grasp her hand, just to know again what it felt like to touch a six-year-old. Will I miss that forever?

I picked up the messages on the answering machine at home and found I had won a local writing contest for nonfiction. I forget what I sent them—some part of Lucas's story. When I first entered three years ago, it was with the story of the children in Vietnam burned by white phosphorus on Christmas Eve, 1968. How strange it seems always to be writing of the death of children. Why have I been witness to such things? When I was young I longed to live an exciting life. I imagined that the death I would defy would be my own. What does it mean that I have instead played the role of helpless bystander to the deaths of innocents, and that whatever courage I have summoned has been simply to endure?

I've nearly finished *Refiner's Fire* by Mark Helprin. It contains this description of a woman:

> Of all her characteristics, the most extraordinary was her smile.
>
> Those with the misfortune of seeing her but briefly remembered her smile for the rest of their lives. God knows where and how it followed and haunted them. The best of gentleness and the best of strength were combined in the beauty of the ravishing lines of her mouth. Her teeth were slightly uneven in the front, so that in kissing, there was character. Even when she wore sunglasses in obfuscation of her gentle eyes, or if her dress were sequined and low-cut, her smile opened up all that was gentle and fair and warm and kind. . . .
>
> Even when partisan for nonsense, she changed it, as if all things were possible, and she often had the effect of making irrelevant his best-protected principles and beliefs, of soothing anger, taming flared passion. . . . Though her external characteristics were splendid and admirable (those fools who think that beauty is nothing are the same as those who think that it is everything), they were best because of their saturation in the light of her spirit.

And so it is with Clare.

AUGUST 22, 1993

Today we again went white-water rafting on the Snake River. Beyond the pleasure of being tossed about and soaked by the rapids, there was a visible sense of the millennia in the limestone of the canyon walls. The brevity of all our lives contrasted with the glacial mountains and timeless river. What conceit it seems to grieve so long for my little boy's flicker of a life. Yet, God help me, I do.

The nights in this place are extraordinary. The sky, replete with stars, appears to yield one up frequently in a dying trail of light. The murmur of the stream outside the window mingles with the sounds of the wind moving though the cottonwoods until it is hard to distinguish one from the other. The geese have honked their way to rest in the safety of some eddy of the river beyond the dike. Only the crows sporadically break silence, seeking, I imagine, one of their kind with which to pass the night.

Memory burdens me like an anchor I cannot raise. It was not always so. My few earthly attachments allowed me to move through the present without fear on the way to a future that held, I imagined, some perfect combination of peace and excitement. That is gone now. I am weighted by the past and advance only haltingly and with great effort toward whatever time is left—full of obligation, but without promise of the joy that I so freely savored.

AUGUST 30, 1993

Something in us dies so the rest can live on, but it must not be the heart.

Barry Unsworth
Sacred Hunger

SEPTEMBER 2, 1993

We came to Atlanta yesterday for Clare's sister Julie's wedding. I feel little enthusiasm for the preparations and so today I flew alone to Jackson, Mississippi, rented a car, and drove to visit my birth mother, Ruth, in Vicksburg. I am adopted and I sought her out eighteen years ago. We developed a friendship and visited back and forth a couple of times a year. Now she has Alzheimer's and is in a nursing home near her sister. Today she looked thin and old. She was able to sit in a chair and have a conversation that made sense about a third of the time; the rest was confused or tangential. She is aware of the memory loss but retained enough contact to ask about "the children." I reminded her of Andrew's and Lucas's deaths and filled her in on the others' activities. Gentle efforts at evoking the past brought forth from her some memories, but most of the time I could not even be sure if she understood who I was. I imagine that our conversation will be quickly lost in the haze of her affliction, but it somehow seemed important to pay her a final visit.

A quote from Sylvia Plath reminds me of Ruth: ". . . I would live my life chastely as a schoolteacher who sublimated by influencing other women's children." This is what Ruth did, moving from grade to grade as I grew older in another family far away. How sad this has always seemed to me, but especially now that we have, I think, said our last good-bye.

SEPTEMBER 16, 1993

This is birthday week: Nina two days ago, Emily today, and Lucas tomorrow. It is a little easier than last year. I thank God for Emily and her amazing spirit.

SEPTEMBER 17, 1993

Happy birthday, sweet Luke. Your Mom and I listened to Ronald Hearn's tape tonight. Even though we cried, we took pleasure in his description of you being happy and close to us.

I think of you every day, but especially this day when, eight years ago, you came into our lives.

Hearn's tape, which he sent us from London in early August, was again eerily accurate ("Lucas seems to be saying something about Gordon and a bicycle") and reassuring ("He's running quite happily all over my flat"). I stare at his "moon" on the ceiling of our room as it fades after the lights are turned off.

SEPTEMBER 19, 1993

Last night we went into Baltimore, to the Tremont Plaza, Suite 2003, and found on its door a plaque: THE LUCAS SCOTT LIVINGSTON SUITE. It was a touching thing for the owner, Debbie Smith, to have done, a sign of her commitment to the memorial even as we continue raising money to finance it.

Jenny, Alec's mother, called from western Maryland. She was weeping and feeling the bitter loss of her son who died three months ago. She asked me questions like "Do you get mad at the doctors?" and "Is it sometimes hard for you to breathe?" I talked to her a long time, read her the Stevenson poem. Her little boy was sick with cancer for half his life before he died. Oddly, Jenny is, as I am, reading Helprin's amazing fantasy, *Winter's Tale*. She sent me a book called *Writing for Your Life*. That, it seems, is what I am doing.

SEPTEMBER 25, 1993

Clare came up with the idea of providing stickers with Lucas's fund's name and address on it for use when people make out their pledges for the United Way campaign. I've done a mailing to all 150 doctors in my group asking for support. This activity has raised my spirits again.

Peter Lake had no illusions about mortality. He knew that it made everyone perfectly equal and that the treasures of the earth were movement, courage, laughter and love.

Mark Helprin,
Winter's Tale

Mark Helprin has articulated many things I have thought and felt on this journey. Though I don't know him, I think I will send him my story and ask if he will write a foreword to the book.

OCTOBER 1, 1993

I have asked a friend for her help in arranging some special event to raise money for Lucas's memorial. She suggested a talk at Hopkins by Art Buchwald, whom she knows. I think this might generate enough money to put us close to our fund-raising goal.

OCTOBER 3, 1993

Last night we served as movie extras for *Major League II* at Orioles Park in Baltimore. We will collect one dollar for each person who designated Lucas's memorial as his or her charity. We worked for weeks to recruit people and the count was around fifteen hundred before the event; I hope they all showed up and signed in. They were still shooting baseball scenes (over and over) when we left at 3:30 A.M. to spend the night with four of Emily's friends at the Tremont. A person from central casting who has taken an interest in our efforts commented that "Lucas never had a chance to be in the new stadium in life, but I know he's here tonight."

I stopped by his grave this afternoon on a bike ride. A thunderstorm was approaching as I sat on the bench we have placed there. Suddenly, from the parking lot near the rectory came the startlingly clear sound of a bagpiper. He was in kilts and preparing to play at a funeral. I almost went over and asked him to play "Amazing Grace" before going into the church, but I feared intruding on someone else's grief.

The kind of hope I often think about (especially in hopeless situations) is, I believe, a state of mind, not a state of the world. Either we have hope within us or we don't. Hope is not a prognostication—it's an orientation of the spirit. Each of us must find real, fundamental hope within himself. You can't delegate that to anyone else.

Hope in this deep and powerful sense is not the same as joy when things are going well, or willingness to invest in enterprises that are obviously headed for early success, but rather an ability to work for something to succeed. Hope is definitely not the same thing as optimism. It's not the conviction that something will turn out well, but the certainty that something makes sense, regardless of how it turns out. It is this hope, above all, that gives us strength to live and to continually try new things, even in conditions that seem as hopeless as ours do, here and now. In the face of this absurdity, life is too precious a thing to permit its devaluation by living pointlessly, emptily, without meaning, without love, and, finally, without hope.

Vaclav Havel
Disturbing the Peace

OCTOBER 13, 1993

When I think now about the fortitude with which Lucas bore his illness and its treatment, I wonder at the wellspring of his strength. The truth is this: in his short life he was never alone and, consequently, never afraid. The result, I think, was an extraordinary belief in himself and us. Even in the ordeal of the hospital after the transplant, his only concern was that the people he loved were with him. He was happy and optimistic because he trusted us and our faith in his recovery, which never flagged until the end.

OCTOBER 17, 1993

The leaves are falling fast now and Halloween is upon us. How Lucas loved that day. Was it only two years ago that he was dressing up as a knight and venturing forth upon the neighborhood with his plastic breastplate and sword—that sword I keep finding in the garage without knowing what to do with it? I cannot throw it away, even though it brings me to tears to come across it unexpectedly.

OCTOBER 27, 1993

I rode out to Lucas's grave today, cleared away the fallen leaves, and washed some spots off the headstone. Then I sat on the bench, watching his silver pinwheel turn slowly in the breeze. The reflection from the early afternoon sun sent flashes of light across the inscription. The impatiens have not yet faded, though they must soon as the weather cools. There is peace in that spot. I feel a kind of acceptance when I am there now: this is where the body of my son will always be. He is not eight; he is still six. Like Ishmael I have survived to tell the tale, but cannot say why.

OCTOBER 28, 1993

Man plans, God laughs.

> Yiddish proverb

NOVEMBER 6, 1993

From *Winter's Tale:*

You can't expect anyone to trust revelation if he hasn't experienced it himself. Those who haven't, know only reason. And since revelation is a thing apart, and cannot be accounted for reasonably, they will never believe you. This the great division of the world, and always has been.

Perhaps, after all, this is the journey that Lucas is taking me on, from reason to revelation. It is a costly trip.

NOVEMBER 7, 1993

I have lived now more than twenty thousand days; Lucas was allotted only two thousand. What have I done with my tenfold more? Not much, I think. Through love I *have* felt the terrible pain of time.

NOVEMBER 10, 1993

Clare and Emily are going to Atlanta this weekend to meet with Clare's sisters and reminisce into a tape recorder about Lucas. I think of them as "dream catchers"—from the loop of willow, its center woven like a web, that the Oneida Indians suspended above their sleeping children. The good dreams were said to flow to the sleeper; the bad ones were caught in the web to perish with the first light of dawn. Clare wept last night as she collected photos to take with her, but I think the memories that come from this trip will help me paint a picture of Lucas and so allow others to know him when he was well.

NOVEMBER 13, 1993

Today, for the first time ever, I cried while doing psychotherapy. The patient was a woman who had sought me out for help to deal with the loss three years ago of her four-year-old son. As she talked about the details of his death, choosing the casket, giving the data for the death certificate ("I should have been registering him in school"), I could not hold back the tears. She also reported a "healing dream" in which she saw her son (who had died in his sleep) again and was able to say good-bye, reassured that he was happy. I envied her this. After speaking with her for about an hour and a half, I was unable to see any more patients this morning, came home, and slept.

NOVEMBER 20, 1993

Now we are in the Bahamas. It makes Emily happy to be back with Kathryn, and Clare and I seem better able this year to absorb the beauty of the place and feel something like peace. This trip marks twenty years since that first idyllic visit here for Clare and me. How could we have imagined the ecstasy and pain that we would experience together? *Had* I known then, I would have given myself to her exactly as I did.

NOVEMBER 22, 1993

One of the things Clare brought down is a wonderful framed photo of the young daughter of a Bahamian friend. The picture was taken by Andrew three years ago. The little girl is standing in the doorway of her house, in a white dress, patent-leather pumps, a cloth flower in her hair, looking solemnly at the camera. Andrew thought it was the best picture he had ever taken. It is impossible to look at the picture, or the photo of the four of us taken on the same trip, without visualizing Andrew behind the camera. I remember Lucas when he was three and four playing with Emily in this room, spinning around, bumping into the bed, both of them laughing.

My problem is one of faith. This is the only life I know—or anyone can testify to. I, like most people, have devoted myself to getting from it as much happiness and as little pain as possible. Just at the point when I felt I had learned what was really important, had in a sense "figured out" what it took to be happy, I have been faced with the loss of two sons. While I knew intellectually that none of us has control over life and death, ours or those dear to us, I thought that the probabilities were on my side that I could grow old in peace, the father of six. I envied no one, saw myself surrounded by generous and loving people, and felt that I had fulfilled my responsibilities to those whom I loved. Now all of that has been turned upside down. I was unable to protect my boys. All that I had and all that I stood for is in question. My work has been to help others comprehend and change their lives. As I try to face my own grief and confusion, I wonder about everything I have done and been. I struggle to make sense out of what has happened, but this feels like yet another futile exercise, of no real importance to anyone, and in the end, a wasted attempt to understand the unknowable. Perhaps, after all, the universe is random and my attempts to attach meaning to it are pointless. My sons may have simply ceased to exist as soon also will I. If I believe that, however, I despair. For the sake of those who still love and depend on me, I must have hope. So I press the search for the understanding I need to go on—but always with my habitual skepticism that I would gladly replace with faith if I could.

A case can be made that we all see life through a different lens. It is this feeling—that my lens has been forever altered—that weighs on me now. Nothing has looked the same to me since Lucas's death. It is the reverse of the moment in *The Wizard of Oz* when everything changes from black and white to Technicolor. For me the transformation has been to shadows of gray in which I struggle to find moments of brightness. They exist, but only in brief contrast to the fog of sadness that envelops the remainder of my life.

Herein lies my quandary: I have tried to live a life of the mind and, in my moment of greatest need, I discover that there is no refuge in reason.

NOVEMBER 23, 1993

From *Winter's Tale:*

Those events which have passed, and which are the foundations of our lives, must be somewhere, he thought. They must be recapturable, even if only in a perfect world. How just it would be if for our final reward we were to be made the masters of time, and if those we love could come alive again not just in memory, but in truth.

NOVEMBER 25, 1993

In this situation, is it simple survival that constitutes victory? Certainly I do not feel victorious. Perhaps, since we are mortal, it is vain to imagine anything more triumphant than an acceptance of our humanity, with all the pain and tragedy implied in that. And a determination to love as well as we can, for as long as we can, those whom God has entrusted to our care.

NOVEMBER 27, 1993

Today we made the long flight from the Bahamas to Raleigh, North Carolina. The first leg, from North Eleuthera to Ft. Pierce, Florida, was sunny, with only scattered cumulus clouds over the long stretches of empty ocean. On the flight to Raleigh-Durham we were on top of a gradually thickening undercast that forced us to eleven thousand feet. Finally, we entered the clouds over the Carolinas. There was a stretch near Florence in which the rain and turbulence became heavy and the little plane, pushed by fifty-knot tailwinds, gyrated through thousand-foot altitude changes from moment to moment. Then we broke out and made a routine instrument approach to the airport in rain and fog. No one was bothered by the bumps. I suppose as long as I looked unperturbed, there seemed no reason for anyone else to worry. Sometimes one flight can seem like a metaphor for my whole life.

DECEMBER 10, 1993

Tonight we watched on television some clips of the making of the movie *A River Runs Through It*. I somehow identify with Norman McClean and his old man's story of a life full of joy and sadness. Memory is both the burden and the grace of the survivor. The attempt to evoke it in a way that touches others is the challenge that helps keep me alive.

DECEMBER 12, 1993

Today I put in front of Lucas's headstone a tiny Christmas tree that Clare had decorated with red bows. I sat for a while as I always do and thought about our unwitting ride to the precipice two years ago. Yesterday, at Emily's request, we bought a Christmas tree for the house. On top is a lighted angel. It's beautiful, and, while the season is still a sad one, I feel we have made some progress in being able to do this much— which we could not do last year.

I also dug out of the garage the rowing machine that we got for Lucas to exercise on when he was undergoing chemotherapy. It was bitterly cold and windy and I really didn't feel like going for a run, so I rowed.

We have made plans for another trip to the Blue Ridge Mountains in two weeks. The skiing will be fun and we won't have to face Christmas morning in a familiar place.

The holiday makes its inexorable approach. I continue my slow climb out of the abyss that swallowed us two years ago. I search, not for an ending to the ascent, but for some ledge where I can rest for a moment. I cling to the rock wall of my life, moving imperceptibly upward, fearing all the time to fall back in an act of futile surrender. I cannot yet imagine a summit, only the painful, unbelayed climb carrying with me the weight of the past. Where are the sunlit plains and quiet forests that I remember? I once thought the mountains of life were behind me, but here I am once more, face pressed against the stone.

Today I went to the funeral of a colleague's wife, dead at forty-five, one year after a bone marrow transplant for breast cancer. There were many people there and a good remembrance by one of her high school teaching colleagues, who ended by saying, "She asked that we take care of one another." One phrase from the priest also stuck in my mind: "Let us proclaim the impenetrable mystery of faith."

We are in the Virginia mountains and Emily and I have had some good moments skiing. She is becoming so skillful now I can barely keep up.

This morning, while standing at the lift building at the bottom of the hill, I was struck by a runaway snowmobile that had just been started with the throttle frozen open. I was hit from behind by the riderless machine. When I got my wind back I thought I was okay and tried to get up, only to have my right knee give way. After a ride back up the mountain on another snowmobile, I am now recuperating on the couch in the condo, getting lots of attention from Clare and Emily, my skiing over for this trip. I hope it's only a sprain and will heal with rest. Emily, who was right behind me when I was hit, is furious and wants me to sue, but I'm not so inclined. Every mistake in life doesn't constitute a lottery ticket in the insurance sweepstakes. I just wish I had been standing a couple of feet to the left. On the other hand, the bindings released, no bones are broken, and I'll live to ski another day. One moment of humor came at the ski patrol first-aid station, where a semiliterate guy was charged with filling out the necessary forms. He asked the requisite demographics: height, weight, date of birth, then inquired, sex? I gave the only possible reply: "No, thank you. Not right now."

DECEMBER 25, 1993

This has been a good day, perhaps a turning point. I lie crippled with my swollen, painful knee. Emily and Clare ski without me. I hobbled out to dinner and tonight we watched the old James Stewart Christmas staple, *It's a Wonderful Life*. Like George Bailey I struggle to believe that my life *does* have importance. I enjoy the love of the two most remarkable people I have ever met. Perhaps I can best handle my grief by paying tribute to Lucas, letting him go, taking my emotional temperature less often, and rejoicing in what I have rather than endlessly longing for what I have lost.

Dear Lucas,

I wrote you last year at this time telling you how much I missed you, especially at Christmas. I still do. I think of you all the time, wishing you were here so Emily and I could teach you to ski. I got run over by a snowmobile yesterday so now I just lie around the condo, reading and thinking about you. There were lots of angel figures exchanged between us this morning, and, while we did not talk about it, you were much on our minds. I hope your spirit is with us and can feel our love and our sadness, even when we laugh with each other. I'm working on a book so that other people will remember you too. In March we are going to open a hotel suite for families with sick kids; your name is already on the door.

I'm trying to do a very hard thing: to love and remember you without getting so sad that I can't be here for Emily and your mom. I want more than anything to be sure that you are happy and safe so I can stop worrying that none of us is with you. I guess I just need to talk myself into believing that you are okay; if you can somehow help me know this, I would be grateful.

Christmas will never be the same without you, but the memory of our time together still makes me feel special. Now I need to give that gift to others, knowing that this is the most important thing I learned from being your father.

All my love,

Dad

DECEMBER 26, 1993

I seem to be recovering; my knee is better, though a pain in my upper back makes it hard to get up and down. I read while Clare and Emily ski. I miss going but try to take comfort in the fact that the accident wasn't worse and that the knee injury is probably not permanent. I regret most the loss of this time with Emily. I imagine that such opportunities will become fewer and fewer as she moves toward adulthood. As with so many other parts of my life, a clock ticks loudly in the background.

DECEMBER 27, 1993

This collision has made me think about Amy's father being hit by the train last spring. At the time I thought there was something self-destructive about his accident. As I try to recover—also from being run over—I wonder at the coincidence. It is hard, though, to come up with much in the way of "contributory negligence" on my part. While I am willing to accept some responsibility for most of what happens to me, I can't really believe that I could have foreseen or avoided that riderless snowmobile.

My forced idleness has had the pleasant by-product of causing me to spend a lot of time in the morning with Emily before Clare wakes up. Lacking anything better to occupy ourselves, we watch the pallid diet of daytime television: "Family Feud," "The Price Is Right," and, of course, the soaps, particularly Emily's favorite, "All My Children." I joke that in the last few days I have lost about thirty IQ points. Because my back injury makes laughing painful, Emily teases me relentlessly with things like imitations of her mom, which are guaranteed to make me laugh. She is such an astonishing combination of caring and ironic humor that I am defenseless before her.

JANUARY 1, 1994

A new year. We are home now and went into Baltimore to stay in the memorial suite at the Tremont last night so Emily could have a New Year's Eve party with three of her friends. Getting off at the twentieth floor I was confronted with "The Lucas Scott Livingston Suite," over which there was a cardboard "Happy New Year" wish. I suppose I need to heed the message: I *can* be happy again, even while not forgetting my little boy. The girls celebrated with balloons and noisemakers while Clare and I had a quiet evening in one of the bedrooms. She is occupied with decorating ideas as we look to the dedication in March. Time is doing its work; I yielded to tears only when, earlier today, I visited his grave, still decorated with evergreens and bows, to wish him Happy New Year.

JANUARY 9, 1994

A friend of Clare's visited again this weekend with her four-year-old son. Tyler slept with his mother in Lucas's room. I read him a couple of Lukey's Berenstain Bears books as he nestled against me in my chair in front of the woodstove. When he was given a choice of people to change his diaper, he asked me to do it and ran upstairs and lay down on Lucas's bed.

Today I received the following letter from Claire Femiano, Lucas's nursery school teacher for two years:

Dear Gordon,

I'm so happy that you will be writing a book about Lucas. To me the book will be about many things. On one level, it's the story of how such a wonderful family pulled together and worked hard to support each other.

On another level, it's about the power and beauty of parental love. When I visited Lucas before the transplant, I was both awed by his strength and inner calm. You and Clare should and *must* acknowledge your contribution to his well-being and peace of mind. He could not have achieved all of that completely on his own.

Gordon, you've often implied that somehow, as Lucas's father, you failed him, that you didn't protect him or help as a father should. Nothing could be farther from the truth. You sustained him and taught him many, many things about strength, courage, and perseverance in a very short time.

You undertook an agonizing journey with Lucas. His story (and yours as the narrator) is as basic, as human, as any story can be—a description of a passage we will all eventually undertake. What is so remarkable is how such a young child could complete it with such courage and quiet determination. It is no surprise that you hurt as you do. You've traveled with Lucas to a place deep and dark in the human psyche and experience, descended so far that the ascent must be difficult. But you *will* ascend, and somehow Lucas and his story will show you the way to the light.

Once the book is written you will, I know, find

solace. From your diary entries, it's clear that Lucas found the light and died at peace with himself.

With love,
Claire

JANUARY 15, 1994

It is cold now, the coldest it's been here in a decade. On my way home from dinner I drove past the church. Sleep escapes me when I think of Lucas deep in the frigid ground and then remember the final events of his life. At some moments I feel like I'm making progress in getting past my grief, then I slip as from a high place and fall back into sorrow. These plunges seem now less frequent or deep.

JANUARY 18, 1994

We received a letter from Art Buchwald agreeing to speak in May at a fund-raiser for the memorial. This is gratifying and the money raised may be enough to endow the suite indefinitely. It's been an arduous task, but we now have about $120,000 collected or pledged. We watched Art on television yesterday discussing his new book, *Leaving Home*. He talked about his motherless childhood, troubles with depression, and attempts to prevail through humor. I think he will be a good person to speak for us.

JANUARY 19, 1994

I was talking with a friend tonight and she suggested that, as adults, we mourn lost children in large part out of our sadness at the future they were denied. The children themselves, however, while young, do not see this as we do. Lucas lived a complete life, albeit for only six and a half years. While I longed to see the person he would become, he enjoyed the present, feeling safe, neither fearing death nor anticipating an existence beyond his family. I mourn for myself and for Emily and for Clare. I am entitled to this sadness but should not confuse it with what Lucas felt and what his spirit must still enjoy: the incomparable pleasure of a lifetime of love, given and received. To weather this loss, to salvage hope, I must perform that task which Christ charged us with if we are to be saved—to see all we have endured through the eyes of a child.

JANUARY 23, 1994

Yesterday I walked in the snow out to the church. I wanted to test my knee, which is healing, and to visit Lucas's grave. It is a barren time of year, though the bitter cold of last week has lessened. Sitting on the bench in the frozen graveyard I felt again a bleakness of spirit, which I am trying to transform into hope and peace. It is not an easy task.

JANUARY 24, 1994

How had this happened? How could grief have taken him so far from shore? He thought of Mattie's face, and suddenly even that no longer served as a bridge. Even if he willed himself to suspend reality and imagine her alive, in her going she had taken something and shattered it, and even her return could not repair it.

Sirus thought of all the phrases he knew, things people said in times of crisis, stories people told to explain life and its problems, but he could not retrieve a single one that seemed to fit. A home is never the same when you lose a child. Was that one? If not, would it now become one, would that be what people would say, long after he and Aileen were dead and buried? Would this very house be a reminder to people of what can happen when a child is lost, of how fragile is the bond between a husband and wife—no, more; between a man and his friends and neighbors, even between a man and himself—that one small child's untimely leavetaking can shatter it all?

Why had no one ever told him this before? Why were there proverbs for everything else, but not for this? Perhaps there was no purpose to having a phrase if there was nothing to be done. Maybe the sayings he remembered were only about things from which you could, with time, recover. This one was left out because it was, at bottom, incurable. He tried to summon God and could retrieve only blankness. Mattie had been his god, his sun, his moon, his reason for rising in the morning, his reason to sit on the porch at night with Aileen. How much of their conversation had revolved around her, what she liked, what she'd done that day, what hopes they had for her future? . . . There was nothing on the other side of her, he concluded, and with this thought, even tears wouldn't come. If he ever felt anything again, he was sure it would be a monstrous fury.

Gwendolyn M. Parker
These Same Long Bones

JANUARY 25, 1994

I had a moment yesterday when I felt as though enough time had passed that I could look back and see the whole of Lucas's life as in an aerial photo. His ephemeral span of time followed long years of which he was unaware, and now this time afterward is lengthening. Looked at from this perspective, the image I have is of a brief and special island of pleasure and hope in my life, the rest of which has been filled with other times and other people, most of whom are still here. I can never forget what he meant to me, but, if I can get at least partial closure on this loss, I yet have some future in which to do something for myself and the ones I love.

FEBRUARY 2, 1994

It is a uniquely human vanity to seek transcendence. If we are fortunate, our lives contain a few such moments; I have had some. Looking back, it seems to me now that Lucas's life provided me with many such flashes of what I could be and do and feel that exceeded anything I had known before or expect to again. I think now that the foundation of these pleasures was not just the intense, momentary delight of our shared affection, but a sense of what we might become together. I would be old, he would be grown. As my life ended I would look at him and see a part of myself carried into the future. This, I suppose, is the closest that most of us come to an earthly perception of immortality. It is a primary reason that we cherish our children. When he died, I lost the comforting certainty that I would live on through him, that his specialness was partly my own and that I would not be forgotten.

In the autumn of my life I was given a son. He was a perfect combination of his mother and me. He had her gentleness and loving heart; he was big and loved to laugh. I was present at his birth and held his hand as he died. My life continues, but I will not cease from longing for what we were together.

Left by Lucas's grave a few days ago was a small flowering plant with this note in a child's handwriting:

To Lucas,
    We are remembering you.
You are sweet like the angels.
We hope you are finding peace
and joy in God's heaven.
                    Your friends

There is a central aspect of this story that has only gradually and recently become manifest. That is, that in the telling I have been, in fact, celebrating—honoring—not only Lucas's life, but his death as well; it is this part of my mourning that has been obscured, even from me, by sorrow. For this loss, which has robbed me of so much and called into question all I am and all I value, has also brought me a deeper understanding of what it is to be human: to doubt, to have faith, to despair, to hope, to endure. To prevail and transcend are tasks that still await me—perhaps in an existence beyond this one—yet I can feel that this is where I'm bound.

Lucas gave me many things in his short life, not the least of which is a lasting sense of myself as a good father. I cherish these gifts and they will always connect me to him. But as time goes on, I am beginning, in a way I never would have imagined, to experience a kind of blessing from his death. I have been humbled, but not destroyed; blinded by tears, but enlightened as well. This knowledge is a clear, revelatory expression of the paradox of grief and joy, which has become for me a natural outcome of and redemption for all I have lost.

MARCH 20, 1994

Today we dedicated Lucas's suite at the Tremont Plaza with an open house that was well-attended by those whose gifts had made it possible. So many people were there who had been important to his life and still are to ours. It was an exhausting but satisfying day. Clare and Emily had done a remarkable job in the decorating and furnishing. The suite looked beautiful and we had collages of pictures of Lucas for everyone to admire. One closet is full of his toys. I hope the families for whom it is a refuge realize with what love and effort that place was created. May they find some peace there in the midst of their ordeals and may their children survive and grow.

I love you, Luke. I would give anything to have you here with us. You wanted to go once more to a hotel. Now there is a beautiful suite with your name on the door. I hope you could see all those people who went there today to remember you.

MARCH 24, 1994

From an editorial in our local newspaper about the dedication:

Lucas was six when he died in May 1992. His small grave beneath the shade of a tulip poplar that blooms each spring at the anniversary of his death bears evidence of love: bouquets and flowering bulbs, letters, the stone figure of a kneeling angel.

Though there is no essential comfort to be had in the wake of such a loss, there is the divine relief of discovering that even in the face of tragedy, all is not lost; there is still love.

Every contribution to the Lucas Scott Livingston Memorial Suite, every gesture of good in a world made sometimes unbearable by suffering, is evidence of faith, the mysterious power that tethers us—more firmly than gravity, more surely than intention—to the world.

CHAPTER SEVEN

dream catchers

From then on I lived at Viareggio, finding
courage from the radiance of Eleanora's
eyes. She used to rock me in her arms,
consoling my pain, but not only consoling,
for she seemed to take my sorrow to her
own breast, and I realized that if I had not
been able to bear the society of other people, it was because they all played the
comedy of trying to cheer me with forget-
fulness. Whereas Eleanora said: "Tell me
about Deirdre and Patrick," and made me
repeat to her all their little sayings and
ways, and show her their photos, which
she kissed and cried over. She never said,
"cease to grieve," but she grieved with me,
and, for the first time since their death, I
felt I was not alone.

Isadora Duncan
from *My Life,*
on the death of her two children

A year and a half after Lucas's death, Clare, Emily, and Clare's sisters, Charlotte, Ann, and Julie, met in Atlanta, where they spent two days together remembering:

EMILY: When you first told me you were pregnant, I was so excited. You came into my room and it was really late and you said that I was going to have a little sister or brother. I remember jumping up and down. I was ecstatic.

CLARE: When we had Emily, she was such a sweet, good-natured child, we couldn't imagine having another baby. And we didn't want to do anything that might cause her any rivalrous feelings or pain. So we agonized about it and put it off until Emily said, finally, that she wanted a little sister. Since I had only sisters in my family and didn't know anything about raising boys, I wanted a little girl too.

We were awaiting the amniocentesis results; Emily was four and a half when we got the call. I was upstairs and she was downstairs; she answered the phone and said that it was for me. I think that she must have guessed who it was because, without my knowing, she continued to listen on the downstairs extension. The doctor said, "I just wanted to say that everything looks great, the baby is going to be healthy, and do you want to know what sex it is?" I said yes, and he said, "It's a boy. Isn't that wonderful?"

I said, "Yes, it's wonderful." Then I hung up the phone and started to cry. I thought, Oh no, Emily's downstairs, I've got to pretend that I'm happy because Emily intuitively picks up every little feeling I have. So I put on a smile, and I went down and Emily was crying on the couch. She had heard! She tried to console me, and I tried to console her. Maybe it will turn out to be a girl after all. Anyway, we can dress him like a girl.

To make ourselves feel better we went right out and bought a little boy's outfit. It looked so feminine that Gordon said, "No son of mine is going to wear that!" It was white, one of those little prince's outfits. We thought it would make us feel better. And then Lucas turned out to be so wonderful we couldn't believe it. We kept waiting for him to be difficult but he had this sweet, affectionate nature. And he nursed in such a special way; he would always look up at me. Both Emily and Lucas nursed until they were three. I remember he was in an observation class at nursery school for two-year-olds, one day a week. The kids would play while the mothers talked about developmental issues. So the mothers would be sitting around and Lucas would walk over to me and climb on my lap and start to nurse, and everybody was so envious of that, of the closeness, and amazed that this gigantic boy was still nursing. He was so sweet about it.

ANN: Do you remember how big he was when he was born?

CLARE: Ten pounds! I had gone into premature labor a month early and there was still concern that he might be small. When he arrived, everybody in the delivery room gasped at his size and then laughed.

JULIE: And when we went to look at Lucas we saw all these tiny little babies and there's this huge boy with his big bruised face and he looked like the bouncer in the nursery. He looked so tough and so strong and so full of life.

CLARE: Whenever we would tell him stories about his being born he would say, "Mom, tell me about when I was a little baby," and I'd tell him that he was so big and he said, "Mom, tell me about when I was *little*." He wanted to be little. Later, when he was six, he became impatient and said, "Why aren't I growing faster?"

EMILY: I remember he would go through these phases of being angry at you for having me first. He wondered why I was older than him and bigger than him. He'd say, "Why is Emily so big? How did she get to be so big?"

CLARE: "Why did you have her first?" I remember him asking that several times.

ANN: I have the image of him on one of his first visits to Atlanta when he had that little tuxedo stretch suit. He would wear it out to dinner; this was before he could walk. He'd be in his little carrier or in someone's arms in his tuxedo and everybody noticed him, he looked so sophisticated. It's hard to look sophisticated at six months, but he did. He'd go out to dinner with us and just lie in his infant seat looking very at ease. When he was little he had curly blond hair. That round sweet face with those bright eyes. He was always a robust little guy.

I also remember when you all came to visit us and we would take these walks in the pasture. It was when I had little Clare and she was as much as I could carry and Lucas was a year older and a lot heavier. I could never carry him because he was so big and I wasn't used to it, but Clare would carry Lucas on these long walks, and I couldn't understand how she did it. I finally realized that it was a feat both of strength and love. I remember thinking: *As your child grows, you just get stronger so that, no matter how big he is, he always feels just right in your arms.*

When baby Clare was in a high chair and Lucas was about one and a half, we visited you, and Lucas was not getting the attention he was used to. You were fussing over this new baby and we suddenly noticed Lucas with his little blond curls over in the corner of the kitchen standing on his head. We realized that he was just trying to be noticed. He didn't act up or try to interrupt us, he was just sweet.

CLARE: His grandmother, Mickey, was so devoted to Lucas. She drove the forty minutes from her house nearly every day to be with him. She left, exhausted, after running around the yard, pushing him on the swing, chasing him everywhere. Often when she left, she would say that she needed a few days to rest, but the next morning she would always be back.

EMILY: I remember when Mickey was with us at a playground. She watched us climb up a ladder to a long, steep slide. Lucas begged her to slide down with him but she insisted she just wanted to watch. Finally, she gave in and slid down with Lucas between her legs. He was thrilled and Mickey pretended to be, although I found out later she had cut her arm on the slide. She never even mentioned it.

CLARE: That was when her emphysema was severe and any climbing was difficult. She would have done anything for Lucas; they were so close. She died when he was two. For years afterward, Lucas would jump up in anticipation at the sound of the front door opening. "Mickey?" he would shout, hoping it was her.

JULIE: You were staying at this hotel on one trip and Lucas was about three. He was running up and down the halls and he put his ear against a door listening to see if it was yours. It wasn't and they opened the door and he went tumbling into the wrong room. They were very glad to see him.

CLARE: I was thinking again about nursery school. We would have nights when the mothers would get together with the teacher and ask about problems and what to do with a child who's resistant, or angry, or starts saying "I hate you." Everybody would say, "Oh, yes, isn't that awful?" I was always sympathetic and pretended that I knew what they were talking about, but Lucas never did that. Everybody else seemed to be having a different experience. For example, neither Emily nor Lucas ever went through the 'terrible twos.' And if I said that to somebody, they would say, "Well, just wait until . . . ," and I kept waiting and they still kept being wonderful. I can never remember Lucas having a temper tantrum.

He slept between us in our bed his whole life. There was something about Lucas that prevented us from ever getting him into his room to sleep. Every once in a while, one of us would say to the other, "Really, it's time we move him." But he was so wonderful to have there because he was so affectionate. Sometimes when Gordon and I would be reading, Lucas would just put his arms around both of our heads and pull us together around him. And he would whisper in Gordon's ear when he wanted him to tickle me, and they'd both start tickling and it would drive me crazy. Every six months or so we would insist that he sleep in his room, but we could hear these sobs, and we thought this isn't making us happy, it isn't making him happy, it's so much nicer to have him here. In the morning he'd usually be asleep holding on to one of us. Since he died I've been so glad that he was always there with us where we could give him everything and get everything from him.

EMILY: Remember after one of those efforts to get him into his own bed, Dad said, "Well, Lucas, how long do you plan on sleeping in here?" And he said, "Oh, until I'm ten."

JULIE: I remember once when we looked for a frog at Squam Lake. We went out with flashlights at night, and Lucas was very interested but scared about snakes. He asked if snakes and frogs lived in the same place. We found a frog and we brought it back to the house and then Lucas got worried about it, and we had to take it back outside. He was concerned about the frog's well-being.

CLARE: Whenever Lucas would have a friend over, and this was true of Emily too, he would end up giving away something of his. I never wanted to discourage this because it was such a generous, thoughtful thing to do, but I would always think, I paid $29.95 for that just last week, and he would be giving it away to a friend. It made him happy. When his friend David, from nursery school, had his sixth birthday party, Lucas was too shy to go but he did want to get him a present. We looked everywhere for this Nerf bow-and-arrow set that Lucas had seen advertised, because he knew David would love it. Lucas and I went from toy store to toy store but we couldn't find one. This was shortly before he got sick. After Lucas died I was going by Toys Я Us and I walked in and they had one, so I brought it home and wrapped it up. It wasn't until the next year that I was finally able to take it over to David.

I talked to David's mother and she said David had been asking for a Nintendo because that's what he remembered doing with Lucas. He said, "I want a Nintendo before I forget the way Lucas taught me to go from one 'world' to the next." So I wrapped up Lucas's Nintendo set and his games and took them over along with the bow and arrow. David was so excited. When he unwrapped the gifts he said, "Lucas knows me so well," using the present tense.

CHARLOTTE: Lucas loved to play tricks on people. I remember that he had that fake pack of chewing gum with the spring on it that would grab your finger when you took a piece. He would get that little devilish gleam in his eye when he offered you some. And when it worked he would laugh uproariously, then a few minutes later he would be back offering you another piece.

CLARE: Once, when he was three and hated going to the dentist, he had an appointment and I reminded him that we had to get going in a few minutes. Then I couldn't find the car keys and had to call up to cancel the appointment. Days later, when I opened the laundry hamper, I found the keys. Lucas had put them there, knowing that this was the last place I would look. I couldn't bring myself to get angry with him; it seemed so clever.

CHARLOTTE: I remember that soon after my mother-in-law died I saw Lucas at his birthday party, and he came over to me and said that he was sorry that Tom's mother had died. I remember thinking that he was so sensitive and mature. Then he asked, "Was there much blood?"

CLARE: Whenever we went to an amusement park, Lucas would see a ride and want to go on it. We'd wait in line for twenty minutes, and when we got to the front of the line he'd say, "I changed my mind, Mom. I think I want to go on *that* ride." And we'd go to another ride, and we'd wait in line and get to the front and the same thing would happen. I remember at the county fair we did that about six times. And you couldn't be mad at him because you could tell, as we got closer and closer, his anxiety was growing. He always thought he wanted to do it but never did.

Santa Claus at the mall is one of the other things we would get in line for and wait and wait and almost get there, and then he'd say, "Mom, I don't think so." Finally, when he was five, he got up the nerve to sit on Santa's knee, but only if Emily would sit on the other knee, which she did even though she felt too old to be doing that.

CHARLOTTE: He was a little powerhouse. He was so strong. He had a big upper body and little tiny hips, the way a football player is built.

ANN: Where was his little stork bite? On his arm.

CHARLOTTE: Stork bite?

ANN: That's what they call them; I call them angel kisses.

CLARE: Do you remember how he would go out of our room past the full-length mirror and just turn around and look? It was unself-conscious, as if he found his image so irresistible he had to smile, or contort his face, or do some gymnastic trick.

ANN: He used to pick those flowers for you from a neighbor's garden and you couldn't bring yourself to tell him not to do that because he so loved to give them to you.

CLARE: Lucas was about four and Emily used to read at night before she went to sleep. I'd say, "Emily, it's time to go to sleep now," and she'd say, "Oh Mom, just ten more minutes." Lucas caught on to the delaying tactic, and if I'd tell him it was time to go to bed, he'd say, "Mom, can I read for just two more years?"

EMILY: He was so strong. Once he was chasing me and I shut my door and locked it. I was chuckling to myself as I walked into my room and I turned around and he was standing right there smiling; he had kicked in the door. It turned out the frame was bent and it hadn't completely locked. It shocked me and I started to scream. I think I scared Lucas because he started to scream too. We were just standing there screaming at each other.

CLARE: I remember how you used to chase each other around the house.

EMILY: I would chase him and we'd run around awhile before I was able to catch up to him. Once he saw that there was no escape, his determined expression would turn into a sweet, pleading face and he would put out his arms for a hug.

CLARE: There was such an intensity in his affection from the time he was a baby. He had a farewell ritual that was so touching. When one of us left the house, he would hug and kiss us and then make us promise to wave to him from the car. He would run to the window and wave until we were out of sight. It was so hard to leave him.

The reunions were equally dramatic. When I picked him up at school, his face lit up; he came running from the playground as fast as he could. It amused the teachers, who joked that it looked as if we were meeting for the first time in years. I sometimes think that he loved us with such intensity because his life was so short.

EMILY: When we were in the mountains in Virginia, my mom and Julie went out to the store to pick up some food and Ann and I were looking after Lucas, who was about two. We got distracted for a minute, and then we couldn't find him. We looked in all the rooms and all the closets; we thought he might be playing hide and seek. We just couldn't find him anywhere, and we were getting frantic. Then I went outside and looked down the road and there he was, wearing nothing but a diaper, crying and pointing. He had tried to chase after Mom's car and had run about a block on the gravel in bare feet. I ran and got him and reassured him and brought him back. I couldn't believe how far he had gone. It was so sad, but we got him.

ANN: You were always protecting him, Emily. One time when Lucas was just a little baby, we were in his room. You kept telling me to watch him, he's going to roll off the bed. We kept saying, "Oh Emily, he's fine, don't worry." Sure enough, Lucas rolled off the bed and made a huge thud on the floor, and he was shaken up and crying. You couldn't believe we had been so careless. He was so lucky to have you as a big sister to watch out for him.

CLARE: Lucas wandered away from us a couple of times in the mall. I always would feel guilty when he disappeared. He thought he was so independent that he would walk off and usually find his way back to us or we'd find him in the toy store. Sometimes he would locate a security guard and they would page us.

ANN: How did he find these people? I never see them around.

CLARE: We kept reading that "Sesame Street" book to him, *Ernie Gets Lost*. And Ernie went to the security guard and found Bert. Sometimes Lucas hid. He would slip between the hangers in a clothes store. I'd look around and start calling, "Lucas, Lucas, LUCAS, LUCAS," and then as I would start to panic, I'd spy the sneakers underneath the hanging clothes. I'd spread the hangers and he'd give me this big smile.

EMILY: He loved pizza. When we were talking about what we might have for dinner, he'd say, "Let's invite the pizza man over."

ANN: Do you remember sometimes we'd be in the family room and we'd be watching something on TV that he wasn't particularly interested in and he would just come in front of us and do a cartwheel; he was really coordinated, I couldn't believe it because he never seemed to practice.

And it was amazing how he could operate all the electronic equipment in your house. He was better than anyone in the family at working the VCRs.

CLARE: He was really smart. I remember his nursery

school teacher, Claire, saying that he tested very high, but she still felt he needed an extra year to get ready for kindergarten. He had this otherworldly quality. Claire said that, socially, the other kids were dancing and he didn't know the steps yet. But it always felt to me like he was on another plane, a higher plane.

Here's an example. Citrina is a little girl who joined the class late the first year Lucas was in nursery school. She was from Jamaica and so cute. They almost had a different language. She was an outsider, so nobody paid much attention to her except Lucas, and he just embraced her, literally. Often you couldn't understand what Lucas wanted to say or what jokes he was trying to tell, and you couldn't understand Citrina either, but *they* could understand each other; they laughed and laughed.

EMILY: Lucas sometimes had trouble connecting with people his own age but not with older kids. He never had trouble with my friends, for instance. Sometimes he was shy with adults, but older kids he never had a problem with. I think he was definitely on a higher level.

CLARE: I think he was astonished by the behavior of kids his age. He couldn't understand why anyone would hit someone else and not share. It was surprising to him because Emily shared everything with him and he couldn't comprehend why other kids wouldn't.

EMILY: He was never mean.

CLARE: After he died and I was trying to find some comfort, I thought that at least he was never forced to confront in a serious way a world where people sometimes behave badly, hurt others for no reason, and refuse to share what they have.

EMILY: I remember Lucas loved *Home Alone*. It was his favorite movie, and I would watch it with him all the time. We could recite whole passages from it. I remember when I was in fourth or fifth grade he got the flu and then I got the flu, so we were both home together up in your bed. We watched *Home Alone* over and over again; we must have watched it six or seven times during the day. It was so funny we never got sick of it; we memorized it.

CLARE: We let him take Coke to school in his thermos. It often got shaken up and when he took the top off at snack time it exploded and went spurting everywhere much to his and everyone else's amusement. Finally, we had to send him with a dime so that he could buy milk.

EMILY: His kindergarten teacher said that everybody wanted to sit at his table.

CLARE: Yes. She said it was because he told jokes. And he would often come up to her and tell a joke, and sometimes it wouldn't make any sense, but she said he laughed so hard that she had to laugh too.

ANN: I was just remembering that Lucas had the kind of laugh that, even if nothing was funny, you just had to laugh too. Some people have those laughs that are contagious. He'd be laughing at cartoons or something really stupid and people would get such a kick out of it.

CLARE: And I remember listening at night after we had gone to bed and Lucas and Andrew would be downstairs together. We could hear the two of them laugh and laugh, and Gordon and I couldn't help but laugh listening to them.

EMILY: I remember Andrew playing this game with Lucas, a telephone game, and Lucas would pick up his plastic phone and say, "Hi, Andrew." And Andrew would pick up a real phone and say, "Hi, Lucas, how are you?" They'd have this little conversation and they'd hang up and they'd take turns calling each other. Andrew would say, "So Lucas, how've you been for the last ten seconds?" And Lucas thought that was so funny; he'd be giggling and giggling. He could make these games go on forever and never get sick of them.

ANN: I remember one trip we took to Hilton Head. Lucas took the greatest pleasure in methodically dropping his toys off the balcony of the hotel, one at a time. What amazed me was that none of you minded at all because it made him happy and wasn't hurting anybody. At the end of the day, you all went down and picked up the toys. It was as if he had just discovered gravity. He was doing a scientific experiment, learning about the world.

CLARE: One time Emily and Lucas and I were crossing the street near the mall. Lucas was between us, holding each of our hands. We took a few steps into the street and this car came zipping around the corner, and we heard this thud and the car had hit Lucas. I was so upset and angry and this guy jumped out of the car and said, "Is everything okay?" I said, "You just hit my son," and I was crying. But Lucas was hopping around, and dancing in the street, and it made me look like a fool. A couple of days later he had these huge bruises. He had such a high pain threshold; he hardly ever cried.

ANN: I remember how attached he was to his little cousin Clare when she was first born. He loved to hold her.

CLARE: It was as if Lucas couldn't get enough affection from all of us. Emily continually showered him with love and held him all the time. He loved having people come to the house. He'd get so excited if any of his aunts or his brothers and sisters came. Outside of the family, he could be shy. But when people he knew came, his energy and affection were boundless.

I remember once we were watching Emily play soccer and Linda, the mother of one of her friends, was sitting on the ground with us on this warm day; she was making a crown of dandelions. Lucas was running up and down along the sidelines the way he always did. And Linda said, "I have something for you, Lucas." And Lucas put the dandelions on his head and then he just grabbed her and brought her face up to his and gave her a big kiss on the lips. She was so surprised. And she still remembers that. I ran into her recently. She said it was one of the nicest kisses she ever got.

EMILY: I remember just before I started the sixth grade at my new school, we invited everyone from my class to come over to my house so we could get acquainted before the school year started. People were really nervous, and Lucas came bounding down the stairs and started dancing and flipping and jumping up and down. It sort of broke the ice.

CLARE: Some of the students I teach at Hopkins, the peer counselors, came to our house one year Christmas caroling. We opened the door and they were all out there singing and holding candles. Lucas asked who they were and I said they were peer counselors; he thought they were my cousins. I guess "counselors" and "cousins" sounded alike to him.

Then we had a retreat at our house with the peer counselors, and Emily, Lucas, and Gordon went out for the day. But when they got back we were still meeting and people were talking about really serious things like how to deal with suicidal students. Lucas kept peeking around the corner to see what was going on. Finally we said he could come in. And without a hint of shyness, he came running in and began twirling around in circles and everybody laughed. Then he said that he could make animal noises, so he started growling and one of the peer counselors made an animal noise. Then Lucas squealed and announced what animal he was going to be, and he'd make this dramatic scene; he just loved being center stage. He couldn't have had a more responsive audience. Everybody was cheering and laughing, "More! Do another animal!" Afterward he kept asking when my cousins were coming back.

ANN: At Squam Lake I remember Gordon reading to Lucas in the evening. I would stand and listen for a little while because I like to be read to also. And they were reading those great "Spot" books and Lucas would pick one out and climb into his dad's lap.

Little Clare and Lucas spent a lot of time outside on the rocks near the lake. They were showing each other pieces of moss or dead bugs or whatever they found; they were always calling each other over to see a leaf. And when we looked out, Lucas and Clare would be holding hands or have their arms around each other.

CLARE: That trip to Rehoboth Beach just before he turned six was wonderful. It was the last trip we all had together. It was too cold to swim, but Clare and Lucas were still running around the beach in their bathing suits and sticking their feet in the water and digging in the sand.

ANN: Charlotte went off with Lucas to the boardwalk, and they were going on those rides. Lucas always wanted Charlotte to be with him on the baby rides.

EMILY: I remember I was doing my math homework one time when Lucas was five. He came in and I was using a calculator and he said, "What's that?" I said it's called a calculator. He said what does it do? And I showed him really simple math problems, like 1 + 1, and I asked him if he knew what that was. And he put up two fingers. And I said this machine does it for you, and I pressed 1 + 1 and he couldn't believe it. He couldn't believe that a calculator did it. He was fascinated; he just sat on my floor playing with it for about an hour. He'd put the calculator down and hold up his fingers and count, and say "I did it." It was great. I ended up giving it to him.

CLARE: Lucas's sixth birthday was the first time that he would let us plan a party for him. Every other birthday we would want to invite his friends, and he'd say, "No, Mom, I'm shy of that." Sometimes we would get as far as making a guest list and then he'd back out at the last minute. But he was in kindergarten and he had really made some friends. Then we decided to get a clown.

So this clown named Smiley came. There was a lot of slapstick. The kids were in hysterics; you couldn't help laughing too just watching them. And every once in a while he would have Lucas, the birthday boy, come up in the center and do something, which would embarrass him terribly. He had a picture taken and made into one of those buttons you pin on. We still have it, and you can see Lucas's shy little face trying to smile; he didn't want his picture taken with Smiley the Clown.

After he was sick, he had to have surgery three times. When he awakened from general anesthesia, he never cried. The recovery room nurses were so amazed that they remembered him when he came back the second time. The first surgery was for the placement of the infusaport; the second was for the extraction of several teeth. I remember when he was regaining consciousness, he had blood all over his face. One of the doctors said he looked like he just lost a fight. And he kept asking for a Coke, but the nurses said "not yet" because they were afraid he would throw up. Finally, they brought him the hospital cola, and when Lucas tasted it he sat up in bed and said, "This is not real Coke!" All the nurses just roared with laughter and said he should be on a TV commercial. This is not real Coke! He can tell! Couldn't pull a trick like that on him! He'd just been through surgery and they try to pass off some hospital cola on him.

CHARLOTTE: Even though everything in the hospital was so intense, when you were there with Lucas it was always reassuring. No matter how bad things were, his spirits were so good. It always made me feel better to visit him.

CLARE: When he was diagnosed with leukemia, he was so interested in every aspect of it. When we explained that the disease was a cancer involving white cells, he asked why they were called white cells. I told him we would find out, and when they made rounds we asked the resident. She looked like no one had ever asked her that before. She turned to the attending physician and said, "Why *is* a white cell called a white cell?" So Lucas would play "stump the doctor" all the time, and his questions would sometimes be hard. He asked for a microscope and we got him one because he wanted to see a white cell. We also put all kinds of other things under it so he could look at them.

EMILY: He liked to look at his hair under the microscope, especially when the chemotherapy caused it to start falling out.

CLARE: He had so many questions. He'd learned about the fight going on inside his body. Ann sent him the germicidal soap and he put it in every bathroom in the house. Of course, it was in the hospital too, and he would make sure people washed their hands with it whenever they came into the room.

EMILY: He was very attentive about those details. Even when he was really sick, if someone came into the room, you'd hear this little voice say, "Don't forget to wash your hands."

CLARE: Our psychologist friend Barbara began coming to visit to talk to him about "the good cells fighting the bad." She used the image of Pac-Man, which he was very familiar with.

We had never allowed him to have a toy gun before, but once his battle with the leukemia started, we bought him an arsenal of weapons. He became this little fighter and he took it on with such enthusiasm and determination. Barbara said that when they talked they had these really intense discussions, with Lucas asking a lot of questions. She did visualization with him, and relaxation techniques that she continued to use in the hospital. When the time came that the doctors said they couldn't do anything else, I talked to Barbara, and she suggested that we bring in home videos of Lucas, for him to be able to see himself when he was well. She said that, even if the worst happened and he didn't get better, his last images would be of those happy, healthy times. So we brought in all these old videos and it wasn't just therapeutic for him, it was good for all of us, to look back and see him dancing in Squam and playing in the Bahamas. And the nurses would come in and say, "Is that Lucas? Look at that curly hair." They had only known him as this little bald, sick boy. We watched them together, over and over again, all those wonderful vacation videos of the happy times.

At Christmas, right after his diagnosis and first hospitalization, we were all there at home. He was on an antibiotic that made him nauseated. He came down and sat on the couch and started opening presents. He was trying his hardest to be happy, but he finally said, "Oh, I'm not feeling too well. Can you take me back upstairs?"

ANN: The next day he felt better. Everybody was with him and he was having fun, playing with his toys; he loved them.

CLARE: I remember him asking for an old-fashioned telephone and we couldn't find one anywhere. Finally we located one in a catalog and had it sent from Michigan. It came the day after Christmas, and so we had to pretend that Santa had returned to make a special delivery. He said, "Did he really come?" He was suspicious.

EMILY: Lucas, Nina, and I decided to give you two a surprise party in the hospital on your anniversary. Nina and I got all the balloons and bought the cake, and it was great. Lucas was so excited about doing this for you guys. While you were at lunch we rushed to get everything ready. "Hurry, hurry, they'll be back soon! Get the balloons, get the candles on!"

CLARE: We walked back into the room and it was filled with balloons. Lucas was jumping up and down on the bed, shouting "Happy Anniversary!"

EMILY: He loved finding Waldo. He was so much better at it than any of us, I couldn't believe it. He'd memorize Waldo books until he could point him out with his eyes closed.

CLARE: Remember we had his Waldo comforter in his hospital room, and at one point decided to take it home because we thought it might be picking up germs? Then one of the doctors who had really gotten attached to Lucas came in and asked, "Where is his comforter?" I said we had been concerned about it picking up germs, and she said to Lucas, "Would you like the comforter back?" He just nodded. And she said, "Get it back."

EMILY: Remember when we had to give him a bath every day in that huge plastic tub. Dad carried him over to it with the IVs connected and we washed him, trying to get the skin to heal. Then afterward, while his bed was being made, Lucas and I just curled up on the futon and watched TV. He was really tired but he could talk; he was so dependent and vulnerable and sweet. We'd watch cartoons.

CLARE: There were two wonderful nurses, Lori and Laura, and Lucas was always so excited to see them; he thought they were so beautiful and so kind. One day his eyes were swollen shut and he very patiently listened to a videotape and talked to me. I asked him if he wanted me to get some washcloths and make compresses so he could open his eyes. He said sweetly, "No, Mom, I'm fine." Then Lori came in and whispered in his ear, "I know you can't see me, but I'm right here, pumpkin. I'm going to get you a drink." As she left Lucas said, "Mom, get the washcloths."

EMILY: I remember when he first needed to come into the hospital for chemotherapy. Michael was there and Nina was there, and you and Dad, and you were all sleeping scrunched together in various places. Lucas and I were awake. We played Nintendo for a while, and then he got bored. So we went down with his IV to the playroom at the end of the hall and played a pizza game for a couple of hours. When we came back, you all were just starting to get up. Then we got him that game for Christmas, remember?

CLARE: Yes, he loved it.

EMILY: He was so good at it.

CLARE: Remember that boy in his kindergarten class named James? He was this cute little boy with spiked blond hair. He and Lucas were complete opposites because Lucas, after he got the hang of kindergarten, was really outgoing and well liked in the class. James was withdrawn and shy and seldom talked. Lucas was so nice to him and would invite him over to put together

Waldo puzzles. I remember Mrs. Kupiec telling us that he would ask James to do things with him to try and get him to open up, and he did. Lucas was like his big brother in the class, protecting him and doing things with him. I remember the two of them together were so cute because Lucas just towered over him.

After Lucas died, James went on to first grade, of course, and one day when I was in the school I saw James and his mother and said hi. His mother said, "Oh, you're Lucas's mother, aren't you?" And she took me aside and said, "I don't know if you know what a hard year James has had; he said that he wasn't ever going to make any other friends because there are no more friends like Lucas anyplace." She said that at one point James got really sick with a high fever. In the middle of the night he came into his parents' room and said that Lucas had been in his room. Then she turned to James and said, "Do you want to tell Mrs. Livingston about the dream you had about Lucas?" He said, "I don't know what you're talking about." She said, "You know, when you were sick." He said, "That wasn't a dream." And she said, "Well, do you want to talk about it?" He said, "Well, Lucas came into my room." And his mother said, "What was special about him?" He said, "Oh, he was an angel." And then she said, "And the next day the fever broke." I thought that was so wonderful that Lucas was still taking care of James. Then I began to think about the effects of Lucas's death on other children. One of his nursery school classmates, David, said to his mother, "I've lost my only friend." And there was a little girl from kindergarten named Anna, who had an older sister in second grade. After Lucas died and she was getting ready to go into first grade, her older sister warned her that it wasn't cool to wear your backpack over both shoulders. Anna said, "I always carry my backpack over both shoulders because that's how Lucas carried his."

EMILY: Remember our visit to his class with the books?

CLARE: After Lucas died and before the end of school, Emily and I were trying to think of something to give the children in his class to remember him by. We also felt that it might be good to visit them and thank them in person for all they had done. They sent so many cards to him in the hospital and even made a videotape where they were waving to Lucas and wishing him well. So Emily and I went through his book collection and picked out a book for each of the children in his class. We wrapped them and took them in, and we gave everybody a book inscribed with their names and Lucas's. Emily and I told them how much it meant to Lucas to have all their attention and good wishes and what wonderful friends they'd been to him, how happy he was when he described them. We reassured them that most of the time he was in the hospital he wasn't in a lot of pain, and was happy, played Nintendo a lot, watched videotapes, and read their cards. Then we asked if there were any questions. One little boy raised his hand and said, "What did the doctors do to kill him?" It was so amazing because I felt like "That's what I'd like to know." When they had last seen him he was in remission. He left school, went into the hospital, and two months later he was gone.

EMILY: On your birthday one year, he wanted to get

you something. He asked me what you liked and I told him maybe we could pick out some soaps for you. He said, "Oh yeah, that's a good idea." So when we went to the mall I ran down with Lucas in the stroller and we got some colored, sweet-smelling soap. Later we were making a birthday card for you, and Lucas went out and asked you if you liked soaps. You said, "Yes, I love soaps," and he came back and said, "Mom likes soaps! Mom likes soaps!" He was so proud of himself that he'd gotten you just the right thing.

CLARE: Just before he was to go into the hospital for the bone marrow transplant, my birthday was coming up and we were in a store buying something. Lucas was hovering around and looking at me oddly. I asked him if he wanted to get something and he said, "Yeah, but I don't want you to see it." I said, "That's fine; the lady can help you. I'll just give you the money and you and she can fix it up." He bought me this little glass angel and he was so proud of it. We came home and he took it right up to his room and hid it. And he showed other people who came into the house that he had it. It was so wonderful. I took it in the hospital with us and kept it up high on a shelf. I thought it was safe but somehow it got broken; I never told him. After he died, one of the first things I did was go back to the store to try to find another angel just like the one Lucas had given me for my birthday. But the store had closed and I still haven't found an angel exactly like it.

EMILY: Remember how upset he got at Julie's birthday when he was in the hospital?

CLARE: Everyone was there and Julie was opening the presents that we had given her. We had gotten a big stuffed animal for Lucas so he wouldn't feel left out. Then he started to get unhappy and we asked him what was wrong. It wasn't that he wasn't getting attention; it was that he hadn't bought anything for Julie. "I don't have anything for her! There's nothing from me!" He was so upset. He turned to me and said, "Mom, get the stroller." His feet were all bandaged, and he couldn't walk. And he said, "Mom, get the stroller and take me down to the gift shop." I told him the gift shop was closed, but I was sure that we could find something here. Julie went into the bathroom so she couldn't see, and we found some earrings that someone had given Emily as a gift. Lucas had never seen them before. They were in a box and they looked new and he insisted on wrapping them himself. Because of the medicine he was taking, his hands were very shaky, but he wouldn't let anybody help him with the Scotch tape. So with his trembling hands he worked so hard to put the wrapping paper around that little box. And then he gave it to Julie.

CHARLOTTE: He was such a fighter throughout his illness.

CLARE: When he was bleeding at the end, in the PICU, and the doctors had tried everything and they couldn't figure out what was causing the bleeding, Barbara told us to speak to Lucas, even though he was unconscious, and ask him to stop the bleeding. We did this, and within twelve hours it stopped. One of the PICU doctors said his wife is a psychiatrist, and he wanted to know all about Barbara and her techniques.

When his blood ammonia rose to dangerous levels and they couldn't do dialysis anymore, the last time that we got help from Barbara was to ask if there was anything more that we could do. Barbara suggested that we just put our hands over his liver and over his heart and say, "Make these places well, Lucas." So we did that, Emily and Gordon and I, and in the middle of the night they got the lab results back and his ammonia level had dropped dramatically. I pointed this out to the nurse and she said, "Oh, that has to be a lab error because nothing can do that but dialysis." But we knew that it wasn't an error. We knew that it was Lucas; he was still fighting. The hardest thing for us was deciding whether to keep encouraging him to fight when it was becoming so hard for him at the end. We could see him struggling and knew he didn't want to disappoint us. So then we asked Barbara what to do, whether we should tell him to keep fighting, which we knew he would do, or whether we should let him go. And she came in to help us that day. She went up to him and said, "Sweet Lucas, I know this is really hard work, and you can do whatever feels right to you."

He was surrounded by so many loving people that last day. We were all there with his grandfather Joe, Barbara and Kirsten and Nina and Michael. Dr. Christensen was there, and my friend Susie came. The PICU staff were so accommodating; they gave us the whole room. Emily was the most wonderful, courageous person I have ever seen. I couldn't do anything but hug him and cry and kiss him everywhere. But Emily had these beautiful memories to share, because she believed, as we all did, that he could still hear us. She told these wonderful stories about all the happy times we had together. Emily, remember the story you were telling him at the end about the sledding? When Lucas was out of the hospital once, we were told not to let him fall because he would bruise so easily. We went sledding by the school and Lucas was just about to go down the hill. All of a sudden Lucas said, "Wait, I'm not ready," so I threw myself in front of the sled doing this split, and Lucas and I slid down the hill like that. Lucas and Emily could not stop laughing. We were all in hysterics in the snow. Emily had this wonderful way of recapturing all these happy times for him. She talked for hours and hours.

Michelle Kupiec, Lucas's kindergarten teacher, told me that when the school was notified of his death she was called to the office and told by the principal that she would have to make the announcement to his class. She didn't know if she could do it, but the principal reassured her that he would be there with her. So, holding hands with the principal and one of the other teachers, Michelle tearfully told the children that Lucas had died in the hospital. Caven, one of Lucas's friends, raised his hand to ask, "Will he be in school tomorrow?"

Once we were visiting Susie in Boston when Emily and I both got really sick. And Lucas went back and forth between us to see if we were okay. Susie would read to him, and then he'd ask to stop the reading and go see how we were and come back. He was just concerned about us and wanted to check on us. After he died, Susie recalled this visit: "Lucas patiently moved from room to room waiting for things to get better. While he was waiting I read him a Dr. Seuss book called *Did I Ever Tell You How Lucky You Are?* It had crazy, wonderful pictures of people in all kinds of impossible situations, and Lucas studied every page with great care. I know that he was thinking how lucky *he* was.

I believe that we are the lucky ones for knowing Lucas. I see him now as I saw him then, sweetly floating to and from each of us like the angel that he was and is, trying to help us feel better."

Now, as with the colored balloons he so loved, I let go of this book, as I released the soul of my precious son, with faith that it will ascend gently downwind, borne aloft equally by my grief and hope. I pray too that there will be those who, facing their own ordeals, will be lifted from despair by the knowledge that love, the truest energy in the universe, is never lost, not even in death.

Finally, the lessons of impermanence taught me this: loss constitutes an odd kind of fullness; despair empties out into an unquenchable appetite for life.

Gretel Ehrlich
The Solace of Open Spaces

THE LUCAS SCOTT LIVINGSTON MEMORIAL FUND

—

As a living memorial to Lucas, we have established a suite in his name at the Tremont Plaza hotel in downtown Baltimore for the use of families whose children are hospitalized at Johns Hopkins Hospital. The process of finding suitable housing can create a financial and emotional crisis for parents already confronting the ordeal of a critically ill child. Since alternative places to stay are limited, this project has been endorsed by the Hopkins Children's Center. Allocation of the suite will be based on need and will be under the control of the hospital's housing office. Additional funds are needed to keep the suite open full-time. Those who wish to contribute may do so through:

The Lucas Scott Livingston Memorial Fund
c/o The Columbia Foundation
10221 Wincopin Circle
Columbia, MD 21044